# DECORATIVE TREASURES from PAPIER-MACHE

# DECORATIVE

# TREASURES from

# PAPIER-MACHE

## by Alice Shannon

with Barbara Shirrod
Photographs by Doug Morris
and the author

Hearthside Press Inc.
Publishers . New York

For my husband

ELWOOD W. SHANNON

whose patience with books
and clutter is beyond belief.

## ACKNOWLEDGMENTS

*Unless otherwise indicated, all projects in this book were made by Barbara Shirrod, craft instructor, for whose assistance I am deeply grateful. Other projects were made by Kay Hoyle, Irene Immerick, Ruth Cadle, Mary Roberts, Helen Gustin, the late Lura Smith, and by me.*

The projects marked with an asterisk are especially suitable for children. (See also list in Index.)

# Contents

# 1.

# THE MATERIALS AND METHODS

This new book about papier mache is presented with the hope that it will fill a gap between the many, which treat papier mache essentially as an exercise for children, and the few, of more recent issue, which present it as the exciting art form it is.

Although I too have included many projects for children (see index for a complete list), all use sturdy durable bases. Why put a lot of effort into making something from a perishable, warpable, leaky milk carton, when it's just as easy to work on wood, tin, plastic or heavy craftboard such as can be found in any household? With these materials as the framework, the finished article is practically indestructible. Even a very young child will be proud when the gift he brings home to mother is sturdy and firm, rather than fragile and, as often happens because of the extreme moisture in the papier-macheing process, warped because its base is soft.

At the opposite end of the gap in the literature is the superb book by Karen Kuykendall: *Art and Design in Papier Mache*. Her handsome sculptures, panels and placques, are the essence of creativity, but they do require a high degree of professionalism from the reader.

This uses only one basic method for most of the projects, Basic Formula I, which utilizes cut or torn paper squares. However, I include three other methods (homemade pulp, instant mix papier mache, and a type involving an armature), for the more ambitious craftsmen.

In the "cut or torn square" method, newspaper cut in squares is the primary material. However, tissue paper, paper towels, Oriental tea paper, gold and silver foil, and other exotic papers (fancy wrappings for example) are used, allowing many variations in texture and effect. Collect quality papers, such as those with a hard finish or linen or rag content; also papers used in envelope linings, gift wrap, and Christmas wrap with metallic finish. Rice paper, and metal foils, will be useful too.

Besides paper, other materials used in quantity are white glue such as Tacky or Elmer's, or any brand of white glue which dries clear; hard-twist chalk line or cord in various sizes for trimming; acrylic paints (these are water soluble and come in all colors, titanium white being the color most used as a base). Two brand names well known for their quality acrylics are Grumbacher and Liquitex (see Glossary). These can be found in almost all hobby shops and art supply stores, and are not expensive, since they are always diluted with water.

Also used are gloss or matte varnishes (these may be diluted with water too). Other materials are gesso, Grumbacher's modeling paste and extender; Gook, a similar plastic paste for building up designs and decorating; gold paints in spray cans or gold, bronze and silver powder; and jeweler's paste to bring out the metallic tones beautifully. Joli Glaze or clear lacquers and varnishes are used for waterproof finishes. Masking tape is a *must,* and for decoration all kinds of plastic and glass "jewels," decorative beads, blobs, medallions, anything you wish to use for embellishment. Bond cement to attach these. Jewelry "findings" for pins and earrings, and small brass hinges and fittings can be found in hobby shops and variety stores.

Very few tools are needed: scissors, a receptacle to hold the prepared squares of paper, a bowl in which to mix the glue (the cut-off bottom of a plastic bottle makes a fine disposable glue pan), small baby food jars for paint containers, 1-inch and 2-inch artist's brushes (inexpensive ones for applying glue), as well as some smaller size camel's hair brushes. A good stapler is important and occasionally you'll use a craft knife, although you can substitute a razor. A card table or work table covered with clean newspapers where your work can dry undisturbed is very handy.

For the basic items to be papier-mached or used in the processes, save plastic bottles of all sizes and shapes, cardboard tubes of all sizes, wooden cigar boxes and candy boxes, tin and plastic boxes, hard plastic items of all kinds (boxes, bowls, trays, baskets), wooden or tin trays, damaged wooden, ceramic or glass bowls or dishes. Anything of metal, wood, glass or plastic can be repaired and glamorized with papier-mache.

And now for those four basic formulas. Remember that they are only an introduction to papier-mache techniques; don't be afraid to experiment and develop your own methods after you've mastered the four which follow.

## BASIC FORMULA I - CUT OR TORN SQUARES

### MATERIALS

> Clean newspapers or other types of paper (such as paper towel, tissue, etc.)
> White wood glue. Tacky or Elmer's are used for projects in this book, but others which dry clear are available
> Scissors, shallow pan or bowl, pencil, carbon paper
> Design pattern, if needed
> 1 or 2-inch artist's brush, soft cloths
> #1 or #2 camel's hair brush
> Preshrunk hard-twist chalk line or cord (white), various sizes
> Acrylic paints: white titanium and colors
> Gold paint or metallic gold, silver or bronze powder, turpentine
> Or gold spray paint or Chromotone gold paint
> Acrylic gloss varnish or matte varnish
> Clear lacquer spray
> Jeweler's paste
> (If you have any question about these products, please consult the Glossary at the end of this book)

### METHOD

1. *Prepare paper.* Begin by cutting clean newspapers into strips, then into squares. Size of squares should be in relation to the size of object being covered, from ¼ inch to 1 or 2 inches. You can tear the paper instead of cutting it if you would like a different effect. Use paper toweling for a rough-textured look. For exotic finishes

use tissue, gold or silver foil or Japanese tea paper. Let your imagination be your guide!

For tissue, a slight difference in technique is necessary. Because of its delicacy of color and transparency, first give the item to be covered a coating of white titanium acrylic paint. This will produce truer colors when you use colored tissue, and will also allow the overlapping of tissue to give additional color.

2. *Prepare glue.* Use a white wood glue that dries clear, such as Elmer's Glue-All or Tacky. Pour glue into a shallow bowl or pan and dilute one-half with water. (Mixing with warm water will give smoother results.) Stir glue and water mixture until it is the consistency of cream. For example: if you use ¼ cup of glue, dilute it with ¼ cup of water.

3. *Applying glue.* With a 1-inch brush, paint the glue mixture onto the area you plan to cover first. Starting at the edge of the article, overlap each square of newspaper a fraction of an inch, dabbing a bit of glue on the square where it will overlap. Be sure

*Fig. 1   Materials needed for basic papier-mache.*

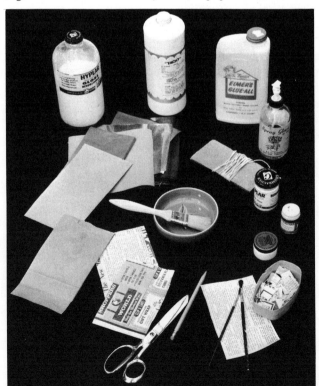

all paper squares adhere tightly to the object being covered. Work out any air bubbles with your fingers.

The way in which you arrange the squares on the object can make a lot of difference in the effect of your finished papier-mache. For instance, you can cover the objects neatly in rows, or in a helter-skelter, hit-or-miss pattern. You can make round, flat trays or the bottoms of baskets or bowls most attractive by placing the squares in circling rows, beginning at the outside edge and following the contour of the basic item. If you are working on a bird, such as an owl with large, round eyes, you can cut paper into small triangular pieces and arrange them in the circle of the owl's eye, pointed ends toward the center. (See the chapter on "Birds and Simple Figures.")

There are also different patterns in which to glue the squares, giving interesting texture and design to the finished piece. These are given in individual projects.

4. *Glue coat.* When you have covered one area with paper squares, coat it with a layer of the half-and-half glue mixture and allow to dry for easier handling before going on to the next area. When the item is completely covered, coat with the glue mixture and let it dry thoroughly.

5. *Prepare cord.* Before applying cord or twine to outline your design, it should be preshrunk, or the drying process, after it's been glued to the item, will cause cord to shrink on the object, pulling your design out of line. Hard-twist chalk line is the best type to use and you can get it in several thicknesses for variation in decorating your work. To shrink, wrap the cord around a glass jar, slide it off and tie in two places, making a neat hank or skein of cord. Drop this into a pan of water, heat to boiling, then remove and let dry before using. This also prevents tangling and you will have fairly small hanks to work with instead of a ball that sometimes rolls away and is difficult to manage.

6. *First coat of acrylic paint.* Before applying the cord, paint the paper-covered object with a coat of white titanium acrylic. Thin it first with water if it is thick enough to leave brush marks. (Acrylics will thicken in the jar after it has been opened.) Do not use the white titanium over foil, tissue or exotic papers as it will cover over their beautiful colors and spoil the effect. When using these special papers, paint the cord separately, then glue it, after it has dried, onto the design which has been drawn or traced on.

7. *Apply design.* When first coat of white titanium is dry (about half an hour), draw on your design with pencil or trace it with carbon paper.

8. *Apply cord.* Use full strength white glue, placing it in a small bowl or pan. Dip thumb and forefinger into the glue and apply a generous amount to a strand of cord, running your fingers down it to saturate it thoroughly with the glue. It is best to use approximately the length you will need for one line of the design at a time, measuring it to the design and cutting off the excess after applying. Exert pressure to the cord when placing it on the design to insure its "sticking" firmly.

9. *Second coat of paint.* For best results, when cord is dry give the entire object including the cord another coat of white titanium, with the exception as stated before of the foil, tissue or other exotic papers. This provides an excellent base for the color which will be added next. Be sure to thin all acrylic paints with water if they become thick enough to leave brush marks.

10. *Other types of design.* If you wish to use a built-up design instead of using the cord, you can use Grumbacher's Hyplar Modeling Paste and Extender, or Gook, the Fantastic Plastic (see Glossary). Some of the boxes in chapter 4, and some of the pins and other jewelry, use this method of design. Extender is also used for texturing surfaces and for giving a smooth finish to styrofoam ball faces.

11. *Add color coat.* Next, paint with the color (or colors if a multi-color design is used), using acrylic paints. Be sure to paint the edges of the cord which touch the paper surface, as otherwise you will find that the white base paint will show. When paint is thoroughly dry, highlight the cord or built-up outlines with either gold paint or jeweler's paste.

12. *Gold or silver antique.* If you would like to antique the entire object with gold or silver as is done in several projects, it can be done very nicely, following this method: Mix gold Venus Bronzing powder with turpentine to make a thin liquid. Apply with a ¼ inch water color brush over the entire object. You will find that the metallic powder and the turpentine do not mix well, and the "separating" process gives a fine "antique" effect. The gold over

white is very effective, also silver over blue. Allow to dry thoroughly. Do not handle more than is necessary from now on until the seal coat is applied because the gold has a tendency to rub off.

13. *Antique color wash.* This is also very effective, giving a different antique effect by using black or a darker color, and is good over foil or other exotic papers. Add water to black acrylic paint to make a thin wash. You may also use another color as contrast instead of black, such as light brown or charcoal over yellow or orange, dark green over pale green or chartreuse - see Apple Bowl, chapter 8.

Brush the wash over the painted or other paper surface, lightly wiping it off immediately with a soft cloth to get the desired antique effect. If you wipe off more than you intended to, brush on more wash and repeat. Don't be afraid to use plenty of the wash; be adventurous!

If you find that the item becomes too dark because the wash was thick, wipe it all off with a damp cloth, add water to thin the wash and apply again until it looks the way you want it to.

14. *Varnish seal.* When all antiquing is completed and has thoroughly dried, coat with gloss varnish or matte varnish to seal. Both types of acrylic varnishes have a milky appearance when first applied to the object, but they will dry to a clear finish. The gloss varnish will have a glossy, shiny surface, while the matte varnish dries to a dull, satiny finish.

If the object upon which you are working will be handled a good deal, it is a good idea to put on several coats of varnish. Be sure to allow time for each coat to dry thoroughly before adding another. Again, as in the paint, if the varnish becomes thick after having been open for several months, it can be thinned with water. The new, freshly opened varnish does not need thinning.

15. *Hard seal.* If after several days' drying time the item remains "tacky" or a little sticky to the touch, coat with a clear lacquer spray for a hard, permanent finish.

16. *Highlighting.* When the item is completely dry, you may highlight the surfaces with gold or silver jeweler's paste if you wish to have gold or silver predominating. Rub on lightly with finger tips, and buff after an hour or so with a soft cloth.

## BASIC FORMULA II - HOMEMADE PULP

MATERIALS

> Large bowl or pail; clean newspapers
> Wheat wallpaper paste
> Wooden spoon or stirring stick
> Liquid bleach

METHOD

1. Tear clean newspapers into bits and soak in enough water to cover in a large bowl or a pail.  Leave soaking overnight.

2. Pour off water, squeezing paper into balls and working the water out of it.

3. In separate pail, mix wheat wallpaper paste with water according to directions on the package.

4. Pour paste into the wet paper mash, mixing thoroughly until it is as pliable as modeling clay.

5. Add one tablespoon of liquid bleach to prevent mould which

*Fig. 2   Materials needed for the homemade pulp method.*

can happen very fast. It is best not to try to keep this mixture longer than a day, as it turns sour quickly.

This material can be shaped into anything you may wish to form, or it can be placed over any type of mold made of material which will not warp during the drying process. When the papier-mache hardens it can be carved like wood, since it has reverted to the wood pulp which paper is originally made of. When it is dry it can be painted and decorated.

## BASIC FORMULA III - INSTANT PAPIER-MACHE

There are several kinds of Instant Papier-Mache now on the market. It is available in hobby shops or art supply stores, and is much easier, of course, than making your own. It eliminates the mess and odor of the homemade type, is much faster, cleaner, and will keep longer. Most instant mixes come in plastic bags, and look like a dry, cottony substance. When mixed with water according to the directions on the bag, they make a good pulp-type papier-mache almost immediately. It can be wrapped in plastic when you have

*Fig. 3    The instant product eliminates most of the mess—and costs more.*

used what you need and kept moist in the refrigerator for as long as a week if necessary.

Basic formulas II and III are used in several special projects in this book and are interchangeable. Two instant papier-mache mixes available are Celluclay and Shredi-Mix. See Glossary.

## BASIC FORMULA IV - OTHER TYPES
## OF PAPIER-MACHE

There are other varieties of papier-mache work; some will be touched on briefly here, and some will be given in projects. One kind uses long strips of newspaper which are saturated with white glue and wrapped over and around armatures (frames) made of wire or wood or chicken wire, even screen, to make figures. The paper-wrapped wire or frame gives the figure body and shape. Before the glued paper dries, the body can be bent, prodded and twisted into the shape desired, and after it has dried, can be coated with the acrylic paints and decorated, following steps in the Basic Formula I. Sometimes sheets of newspaper or other papers are merely glued, then wrapped and bunched over the wire "skeletons."

Papier-mache figures that will become collector's items are given in chapters 9 and 10. These are usually made over an armature, using cloth or paper saturated with glue, the folds of the draperies arranged while the material is wet, then spray painted with gold when dried. After the basic figure and draperies are dried, costumes made of velvet and silk, trimmed with gold braid, beading, jewels and so on can be added. These are actually works of art and collectors are beginning to acquire them. They will in time become heirloom pieces if cared for properly.

# 2.

## MATCHING BATH ACCESSORIES

For a first project in papier-mache craft, three matching items, a wastebasket, tissue box cover and spray can cover, will prove to you how easy it is to use the "cut square" method, Basic Formula I, and

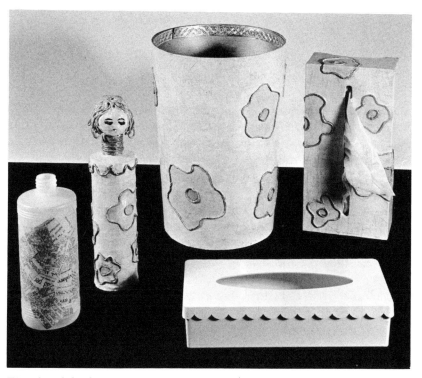

*Fig. 4    A bath accessory set, before and after.* Made by Lura Smith.

will also add high style to your bathroom. The set shown in figure 4 was done in ivory with yellow free-form flower designs outlined in gold cord. But use colors that match or contrast with your own bathroom, and use your own free-form or traced designs. Butter-flies, poodles, fish, shells, flowers, kittens, zoo animals, are fun to do.

## WASTEBASKET

### MATERIALS

> Craftwood or ice-cream carton or plastic wastebasket, any size, or an old one of any material
> White glue
> Clean newspaper, scissors, small shallow bowl or pan
> Hard-twist cord or chalk line
> White titanium acrylic paint—see Glossary
> Colored acrylic paints of your choice, #1 or #2 artist's camel's hair brushes
> 1-inch paint brushes for glue—inexpensive ones that can be thrown away later
> Gold spray paint, gold braid 1 inch wide, Bond cement
> Chromotone gold paint, acrylic gloss varnish
> Gold jeweler's paste
> Clear lacquer spray

### METHOD

A two-gallon craftwood carton was used to make the wastebasket shown in this project. But you can use an inexpensive plastic waste-basket or an old wooden or metal one. Be sure the surfaces on both the inside and outside are clean before you begin.

1. First paint the inside of the wastebasket, using gold spray paint or a contrasting color, or even papier-mache the inside if you wish.

2. Decide on the size of squares you wish to use. The ones used here are 2 inches by 2 inches. Cut 2-inch strips of newspaper lengthwise, then cut the squares into a handy small box or receptacle (shoe boxes are good). Cut several folds of the newspaper at a time. Check Basic Formula I before beginning.

3. Prepare glue in a small, shallow bowl or pan by diluting one-half with water, mixing so that it is the consistency of cream. The

cut-off bottoms of plastic bottles make very good glue dishes which may be thrown away when you are through with them.

4. Use a 1-inch paint brush to apply the glue. The brush does not necessarily have to be an expensive camel's hair brush, but with proper care the glue can be washed out with cold water, and the brush used again and again. However, when it does become matted and gummy it should be thrown away. The same is true of brushes used with the acrylic paints, since they are water soluble and can be washed out with cold water. With a bit of care, your brushes can be used many times.

Paint the glue mixture over the area you first plan to cover, not the entire basket or it will dry before you get the squares placed. Starting at the top edge of the wastebasket, place the paper squares on the glue surface, overlapping each square a fraction of an inch or more, if you wish. (Read Basic Formula I, chapter one, very carefully before beginning work, although some of the projects will vary slightly in method for different reasons.) The wastebasket in figure 5 was done in a hit-or-miss pattern which added interest to

*Fig. 5    Start at the top and overlap each square.*

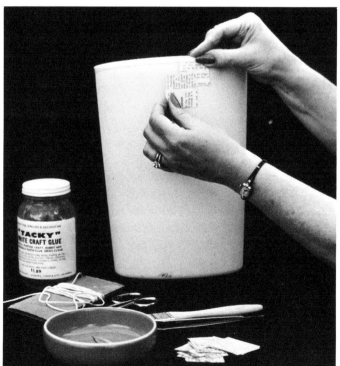

the overall effect. After each square is placed, dab a bit of glue where the next one will overlap so you will have a complete seal. Be sure you cover every bit of the wastebasket, so that there are no gaps, and all squares are tightly adhered.

When the first area is covered, coat the squares with glue and go on to the next area, repeating these two steps until the entire outside is completely covered. Now, give the paper squares another coating of glue so that you can be sure the paper is solidly adhered. Dry overnight, or until thoroughly dry. Turn upside down, covering bottom of the wastebasket in the same way as above. Allow to dry thoroughly.

5. Now paint the entire paper-covered outside of the basket with white titanium (this is the name of the basic white color) thinning it with water if at first the brush leaves marks.

6. In about one-half hour it will be dry enough so that you can draw on your design with pencil, or trace it with carbon paper.

7. Prepare cord, pre-shrinking it as in Basic Formula I, step 5. The cord varies in size, even on individual objects, depending on its purpose in the design. Fairly thick cord was used for this project. Use full-strength glue. Apply the saturated cord firmly over the design outlines, exerting pressure with your fingers to be sure it will adhere firmly.

8. When the glued cord has dried thoroughly, give the entire paper surface of the basket, including the cord design outlines, another coat of the white titanium acrylic paint. Let dry.

9. Now paint in the background color, being careful to paint the cord edges next to the paper surfaces. Paint inside the cord outlines next with the colors you have chosen for your design, carefully painting the color into the base of the cord inside the design. Remember to thin the paint if it has thickened enough to leave brush marks.

10. When the colors have dried sufficiently, paint the cord outlines with Chromotone (see Glossary) gold paint, using a #1 or #2 camel's hair artist's brush. Or you may rub the cord with gold jeweler's paste applying with the finger tip.

11. Antique wash. A light charcoal grey, very thin wash, was used on the ivory and yellow wastebasket shown. See step 13 in Basic Formula I for instructions on various washes to use for antiquing.

12. When all paint is thoroughly dry, apply an overall coat of

acrylic matte or gloss varnish to seal. This looks milky when it goes on, but dries to a clear finish. (See step 14 in Basic Formula I.)

13. When varnish is dry, apply a coat of clear lacquer spray for a hard, waterproof finish.

14. For the finishing touch, glue 1-inch wide gold braid around the inside rim of the wastebasket using full-strength white glue.

## MATCHING TISSUE BOX COVER

This pretty accessory was made from a wooden box top which fits over the ordinary tissue box. A slot ½ inch wide and 8 inches long was cut in the top for the tissues to pop through. However, you can buy a plain plastic one at a variety store if you don't have a box top the proper size.

### MATERIALS

The materials will be the same as for the wastebasket (see preceding project), using colors and design to match it

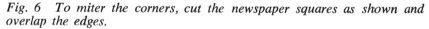

*Fig. 6   To miter the corners, cut the newspaper squares as shown and overlap the edges.*

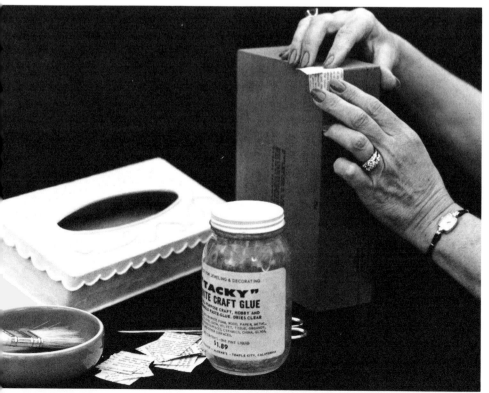

METHOD

1. Prepare somewhat smaller newspaper squares for this - about a 1½-inch size was used for the one illustrated.

2. Apply paper squares with diluted white glue mixture as in wastebasket. For neat edges on the square corners of the box, you may have to cut a slash in the paper square and lap it over smoothly. Coat with glue when completely covered, and dry.

3. Give first coat of white titanium. This should be dry in about half an hour.

4. Pencil or trace design.

5. Glue pre-shrunk cord over design outlines, using full-strength glue.

6. When dry, apply another coat of white titanium, covering cord and paper squares completely. Allow to dry.

7. Paint with colors matching wastebasket designs, making sure the base of cord is covered with color. Otherwise the white will show through.

8. Paint cord outlines with gold as in wastebasket.

9. It is not necessary to paint the inside of the cover unless you wish to, since it will not be seen. However, the unfinished wooden underside of this one was painted with black gloss enamel.

*Fig. 7   The jeweled tissue box outlined in cord.*

10. Apply antique charcoal wash, or other color wash. (See step 13, Basic Formula I.)

11. When all paint is well dried, apply a coat of acrylic gloss varnish or matte varnish to seal.

12. When this is dry add a coat of Joli Glaze or clear lacquer spray for waterproofing. As soon as this has completely dried, the cover may be placed over a tissue box.

## SCALLOPED HINGED TISSUE BOX

This receptacle for your tissue boxes is lovely and practical too since it hangs on the wall.

### MATERIALS

Same as preceding tissue box—except for the addition of glass jewels

### METHOD

Same as preceding tissue box, except that you glue cord on lid outlining scallops. When finished, glue glass jewels in attractive pattern to top.

## MATCHING PIXIE SPRAY CAN COVER

This is adorable and can be used to cover a hair-spray can or bathroom deodorizer can. The complete 3-piece set of bathroom accessories is high fashion, and no one will dream it was made from odds and ends.

### MATERIALS

Plastic starch container bottle or any plastic bottle which will fit nicely over your hair spray can or whatever you intend covering with it

This one was approximately 7 inches high

Styrofoam ball about 2½ inches in diameter for head

Cardboard strips, masking tape

Cord or twine, pre-shrunk, finer for neck, heavy for hair and scallop outline

Gesso

Other materials as for wastebasket (newspaper, glue, etc.)

METHOD

1. Cut off bottom of plastic bottle.

2. Prepare ½-inch newspaper squares or a bit larger.

3. Glue on squares using brush with glue and water mixture as in basket. To make the squares fit the rounded shoulders of the bottle neatly, cut top edge of squares in slashes about 1/8 inch or smaller and you will find that the paper will fold nicely to fit the rounded edges. The squares were placed in even rows around the bottle, not in a hit-or-miss arrangement as in the other two pieces.

4. Make neck. Form a cardboard tube 1¼ inches long and about 1 inch in diameter or whatever size is needed to fit around bottle neck and cap. Glue around the outside edges of the bottle cap and neck, then wrap it securely with masking tape, or glue strips of paper around it to hold firmly. Glue on the styrofoam ball for the head, using full-strength glue for both neck and head joinings. With full-strength glue saturate cord with fingers and wrap firmly around neck in several layers to completely cover.

5. Coat with diluted glue mixture and allow to dry thoroughly.

6. Give first coat of white titanium, making sure paint is not too thick.

7. When dry, pencil or trace on design, drawing a border of scallops just below "shoulders" of figure.

8. Apply heavier cord to design outline, using full-strength glue and pressing firmly. Allow all to dry.

9. Paint entire figure, including head, with white titanium. Dry.

10. If face is not smooth after painting with white titanium, give it a coat of Gesso and allow to dry.

11. When dry, glue loops of the heaviest cord onto head for hair, saturating cord with full-strength glue and modelling the hair as you want it to look when finished since it will dry stiff.

12. Paint with colors to match wastebasket and tissue box cover, using acrylic paints.

13. When all is dry, paint the hair bright yellow or any color you prefer. Paint face with flesh tone acrylic paint, and when dry, paint on features.

14. Add charcoal grey antique wash to body of bottle if desired.

15. Paint all cording in design with gold paint or use jeweler's paste. Dry.

16. Finish when thoroughly dry with sealer coat of acrylic gloss varnish over all.

17. For waterproof, non-sticky coat, add Joli Glaze or spray with clear lacquer when sealer coat is dry.

18. The inside does not require finishing.

# 3.

## FOR BEDROOM AND BOUDOIR

Pretty and practical items can be used very decoratively in the bed-room. Here are some delightful articles to bring color to the master bedroom, guest room, and even a child's room. They are very simple to make, require few materials and are marvelous gifts for those people who have "everything."

### "LITTLE GIRL" FIGURINE SPRAY-CAN COVER

This pretty little figure, pictured both in black and white (figure 8) and in color, was created by Lura Smith who molded the adorable little head with Hydrastone casting powder. You may do this also, if you wish, but plaster and plastic heads are available in art supply stores and hobby shops.

MATERIALS

> Liquid soap plastic bottle, large enough to cover spray can
> Plaster head, masking tape
> Newspapers, white glue
> Paint brushes
> Acrylic paints: white titanium, pink or flesh-tone, lavender, yellow, black and burnt umber
> Acrylic gloss varnish

Clear lacquer spray
Cotton rickrack or fancy braid; textured wallpaper; paper lace doily
   or wide ribbon for shawl; artificial forget-me-not spray
Gold paint

METHOD

1. Cut off top of plastic bottle. An X-Acto craft knife is good for this, but good, sharp scissors will do.

2. Attach head with masking tape to bottom of bottle, wrapping the tape securely and smoothly so that head will not wobble and neck will be smooth.

3. Cut newspaper squares and completely cover the plastic bottle, using diluted glue as in Basic Formula I. You will notice in the illustration that the squares have been applied in a hit-or-miss fashion. Be sure to cover the raw edges of the bottom with the paper squares. Do this by slashing the bottom half of each square and folding it neatly over the edge. When completely covered with paper, brush on a coating of glue and allow to dry thoroughly.

*Fig. 8 Spray-can cover topped by "little girl" figurine, see also Color Plate X.*

4. Paint entire figure including plaster head with a coat of white titanium. Let dry.

5. With full-strength glue, attach rickrack or braid to shape the low neckline. Cut and fold the textured wallpaper or paper lace doily or use wide ribbon to form a dainty shawl which will come to a point in front, covering her non-existent "hands." Glue shawl in place with full-strength glue.

6. When all is dry, mix a small amount of lavender acrylic paint with white titanium to obtain a delicate lavender-orchid for the dress. Paint dress area and braid neckline, then mix a deeper lavender tone for the shawl. Paint shawl and allow figure to dry.

7. Mix flesh tone or pink and tint the face and neck. Allow to dry before painting hair.

8. Mix yellow and burnt umber to get golden hair color; paint hair. Dry.

9. Paint features.

10. Make gold wash as in Basic Formula I, step 12. Apply and lightly wipe off to get desired antique effect.

11. Cover entire figure with gloss varnish. Let dry, then highlight with gold jeweler's paste.

12. Glue artificial flower spray to point of shawl for her "nosegay."

## "LOVELY LADY" SPRAY CAN COVER

This pretty dressing table accessory (figure 9) is even simpler to make than the one just described and it is also larger.

MATERIALS

    Heavy cleaner's cardboard tube (container for plastic garment bags)
    Plaster of Paris head to fit tube, masking tape
    Acrylic paints: white titanium, black, burnt sienna, burnt umber, flesh
    Clear plastic spray, lacquer spray
    Wallpaper scraps; heavily textured and figured gift wrap paper
    White glue
    Gold spray paint

METHOD

1. First spray both the textured wallpaper and the gift wrap with gold spray paint before using. Place sheets of paper in the

*Fig. 9 "Lovely Lady" spray can cover,* by Kay Hoyle; *gluing yarn "hair" on wooden spoon mirror.*

bottom of a deep cardboard box, take out of doors and spray. Do not breathe spray fumes or try to spray if the wind is blowing.

2. Attach plaster of Paris head to one end of cardboard tube with masking tape smoothly so that no ridges will show.

3. Cover entire tube with the dried, sprayed wallpaper using full-strength glue. Be careful to cover the bottom edges of tube by extending the wallpaper below the edge, slashing with scissors all the way around, then folding and gluing to the inside of tube.

4. Fold gold-sprayed, flowered gift-wrap paper into pleats and glue down the front length of the figure. With more of the gift wrap, form sleeves from the "shoulder" of the figure to center front, checking with figure 9; make a flared ruffle at the "wrist" by forming three pleats at the elbow and fanning them out at the wrist.

5. Cut out a hand from plain white paper; paint flesh-colored or eggshell; draw lines suggesting fingers; insert hand at end of sleeve. (Make flesh color by adding pink to white titanium; eggshell by adding brown to white titanium.)

6. Paint neck and face with flesh-toned or eggshell acrylic.

7. When dry, paint features: eyes blue, eyebrows black, pink

31

mouth. Paint hair with a mixture of white titanium and burnt sienna. Dry.

8. When thoroughly dry, antique the hair, using a wash of burnt umber, wiping skillfully, so as to highlight the hair. Allow to dry.

9. Make pleated ruffle about 1½ inches wide of the gift-wrap paper and glue to the top of tube so as to cover about 1 inch of the tube and ½ inch of neck. This creates the pleated "collar" effect.

10. When dry, coat with matte varnish, covering the entire figure. Allow to dry.

11. A coat of clear lacquer may be applied if desired for harder seal.

12. Highlight with gold jeweler's paste.

## HIGH-STYLE GOLD HAND MIRROR

This exquisitely beautiful hand mirror, a true "objet d'art," can be made from an old battered mirror that has seen better days or from an inexpensive plastic one from the five-and-dime.

MATERIALS

> Hand mirror
> Clean newspaper squares or paper towel squares for textured effect
> Pre-shrunk, hard-twist cord; white glue
> Gutta-percha or simulated wood carved medallion (Glossary)
> White titanium acrylic paint, acrylic gloss varnish
> Gold jeweler's paste; soft cloth

METHOD

1. Cut newspaper squares or toweling to size desired and glue to back, front rim, and handle of mirror, using diluted glue. Begin at outside edges and work to the center. Turn edges carefully, using "fringing" method. The neatness and artistry with which the paper squares are glued on will have everything to do with the total effect of the finished mirror, so take great pains with this step. When completely covered, coat with glue and allow to dry thoroughly.

2. Using full-strength glue, place cord on mirror, making a border on the back about 1 inch from the edge (see figure 10) and another border framing the mirror. Glue the cord in a design to outline the mirror handle if it is flat and wide enough to do so. Wrap

*Fig. 10   Finish the mirror by rubbing it with gold jeweler's paste (see Glossary).*

several strands of cord around the point where handle and mirror join, making a loop as in the illustration. Press the glue-saturated cord firmly to the papered surface with fingers as in Basic Formula I instructions. Allow to dry thoroughly.

3. When fully dry, coat with white titanium, covering cord and paper surfaces completely.

4. Glue simulated wood-carving figure or medallion to center back of mirror with full-strength white glue. A lovely figure of a goddess (perhaps Venus or Diana) could be used for this mirror, but other possibilities such as medallions, flowers, bows or swags, are illustrated. Use your imagination. If you cannot obtain the simulated wood carvings, a circlet of jewels would be effective, but do not glue on jewels until all other steps are finished.

5. Apply gold jeweler's paste to surfaces of hand mirror with fingers, giving it a rich gold color, rubbing the paste well into the cord, especially at the base line so that no white will show. Allow to dry, then buff with soft cloth.

6. Brush with a coating of gloss varnish. Dry.

7. If desired, touch up top surfaces of cord and the simulated wood carvings with the gold jeweler's paste.

### WOODEN SPOON MIRROR

Whimsical mirrors made of wooden spoons, large or small, appeal to youngsters and will brighten any room. Barbara Shirrod created these sparkling decorations with a girl's face as well as a clown face.

**MATERIALS**

Any size wooden spoon
½-inch or 1-inch newspaper squares, depending on size of spoon
White glue; pre-shrunk, hard-twist cord
Oval mirror to fit spoon bowl
Acrylic paints: white titanium, Hooker's green, cadmium yellow, flesh-color or pink, black
Small bowls for paints and glue, brushes
Acrylic matte varnish
Small picture hanger

**METHOD**

1. Cover entire spoon with torn newspaper squares, brush on a coat of the diluted glue and allow to dry thoroughly. Check directions for Basic Formula I before beginning.

2. Using full-strength glue to saturate cord as directed, outline spoon with cording. Form girl's hair with cord or outline the clown's cap (see figure 9) on back of the spoon, pressing cord down

*Fig. 11 Making a border around the back of the hand mirror.* By Lura Smith.

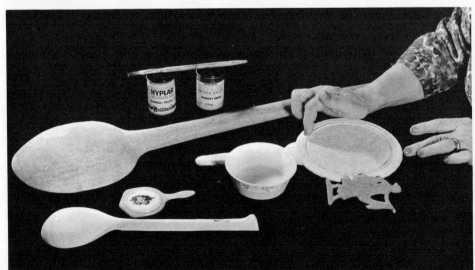

firmly with finger. Also form a collar at the base of spoon between the bowl and handle. Make a half-daisy at the base of collar, extending to the edge of the spoon.

3. Fit oval mirror into the curved bowl of spoon, gluing firmly with full-strength glue. Outline the edge of mirror with cord. Allow to dry thoroughly. *Note*: If you cannot find the proper size mirror to fit your spoon, an old mirror can be cut by an experienced person using glass or tile cutters.

4. Paint the entire spoon including cord, but not the mirror surface of course, with white titanium. Let dry.

5. When dry (it should dry in less than an hour) tint face with flesh tones or pink. Dry.

6. Paint "hair" with cadmium yellow or desired color. Paint inside cord outlines of clown hat.

7. Paint front and back surfaces of handle with Hooker's green. When green is dry, dip a cotton ball into yellow, shake off excess and dab spots of yellow color over the green surface to tie in colors.

8. Paint on the features in desired colors. If making a clown, paint round pink spots on his cheeks, outline a large red mouth with white, and paint clown features. Glue on a round red nose. Let your imagination be your guide.

9. When mirror is finished to your satisfaction and well dried, brush over the painted surfaces with matte varnish. Let dry.

10. Tack a small picture hanger just above the top of the mirror so that the spoon "face" will show. You can glue on a hanger if the edge is too narrow.

11. Highlight cord with gold jeweler's paste.

## JEWELED STANDING MIRROR

This jewel-encrusted mirror is one of those elegant and beautiful accessories that you can always find place for on your dressing table, night stand, or even hanging on the wall. It is easy to make and a most rewarding project.

MATERIALS

> Inexpensive standing-frame mirror or use plywood square on which you have glued a small mirror
> Newspaper, white glue

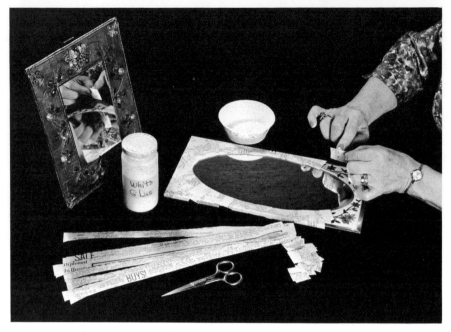

*Fig. 12 Making the jeweled standing mirror.* By Lura Smith.

Small bowl, brushes
Preshrunk cord
Acrylic paint: white titanium, blue
Gold jeweler's paste
Metallic gold leaves, multi-colored glass jewels
Bond cement

METHOD

1. Cut newspaper into 1-inch squares or larger, depending on size of the mirror frame to be covered.

2. With diluted white glue begin at center edge of mirror, gluing squares in overlapping rows around edges of mirror until the entire background framing the mirror is covered. Cover edges of frame, too, turning squares under, neatly. Allow to dry.

3. Using full-strength white glue, place cord on mirror in the desired design. (See figure 12 of finished mirror for patterns.) Be sure the loops of cord are large enough for the jewels to fit into later. Outline mirror with cord, and also the edges of frame. Allow to dry thoroughly.

4. When dry, coat entire newspaper-covered surface and cord with

36

a layer of white titanium paint. Let dry.

5. Give one coat of blue acrylic paint. Let dry.

6. When entirely dry, cover with gold jeweler's paste. Buff with soft cloth when paste is dry to remove excess gold.

7. Place jewels and metallic gold leaves in place with Bond cement.

8. If mirror back needs color, paint it with blue acrylic paint and tone with gold jeweler's paste when dry.

## INSTANT PAPIER-MACHE WASTEBASKET

A dainty basket for the bedroom with a matching vase (next project). You can make this imaginative gift—for pennies.

MATERIALS

> Instant papier-mache: Celluclay, Shredi-Mix or other (see Glossary)
> Large bowl, wooden spoon or stick
> A base which flares to the desired shape (see figure 13). This can be a round, oval or square wastebasket, either new or used, but it must be tapered, so the papier-mache shell will slide off the smaller end when hardened. The base mold may be used many times.
> Aluminum foil, cord, white glue
> White titanium acrylic paint
> Gold jeweler's paste, Gook or Magic Steel (see Glossary)
> Clear lacquer spray or Joli Glaze
> Butterflies (natural wings, paper bodies)

METHOD

1. Read Basic Formula III in chapter 1 on Instant Papier-Mache before beginning this project. Follow manufacturer's directions as some are mixed differently than others.

2. Pour about 1 pound of the mix into a large bowl, adding the required amount of water. Mix until it is the consistency of soft putty.

3. If the base form is made of lightweight cardboard or any porous material, aluminum foil should be used over it so that the papier-mache shell will not stick to it. Place the foil over the outside of the basket, covering it as smoothly as possible.

4. Pat the papier-mache mixture over the outside surface of the base form, making a layer about ¼ to ½ inch thick. You can tex-

*Fig. 13   The "instant" wastebasket and matching butterfly vase.*

ture the surface or smooth it, whichever you wish—it's a little like
playing with mud pies! The surface will dry in the texture you give
it in about 24 hours or longer, depending on thickness of the layer.
When dry it will be firm and hardened and will pull away from the
model form easily.

5. Remove dried shell from base form. It should slide off easily.
If the edges crack or break, don't panic. Merely mend it with
more wet papier-mache mix after removing it completely, and allow
the mend to dry before starting work on it.

6. When thoroughly dry, paint inside and out with white titanium
acrylic paint. Let dry.

7. Apply Gook or Magic Steel directly from the tube to make
the design; in this one, a vine and leaf effect spirals around the

basket. Allow to dry thoroughly.

8. Brush on a second coat of white titanium. If color other than white is desired, brush this on when the second coat of white is dry.

9. Highlight the raised design of vine and leaves with gold jeweler's paste. Coat with Joli Glaze.

10. Carefully place butterflies in position on the wet glaze, coating the butterfly with glaze with the brush to hold it in place. The glaze will also act as a protective material on the delicate wings.

11. Allow to dry thoroughly, then coat inside of wastebasket with Joli Glaze.

## *MATCHING BUTTERFLY VASE

Pretty and practical, this vase is lots of fun to make. Perhaps a small daughter or son would enjoy doing it while you make the wastebasket.

MATERIALS

Plastic bottle (wide-mouthed type used for bath salts, liquid soap or similar product—see figure 13)
Same materials and decoration as wastebasket in preceding project

METHOD

1. Mix the Instant Papier-mache as per directions on the container.

2. Pat a layer of the mix over the plastic bottle and give it a texture similar to the wastebasket.

3. Allow to dry. Do not remove from the bottle base as was done with the wastebasket. The bottle will hold water for fresh flowers.

4. Finish the vase in the same way as wastebasket, using Gook or Magic Steel for design and adding smaller size butterflies as in step 10.

5. Do not coat inside of vase.

## HANDSOME WIG STAND

Every lady needs a wig stand these days, but none of the ones that come with hair pieces are as decorative as this one.

MATERIALS

> Sculptured styrofoam head (very inexpensive)
> Heavy wood block for stand
> Newspaper, glue
> Acrylic paints: white titanium, black, brown, red, flesh-tint, yellow
>     if desired
> Acrylic gloss varnish, .00 camel's hair artist's brush

METHOD

1. Cut 1- or 2-inch newspaper squares into equilateral triangles, so that all three sides measure the same. Triangles are easier to use on the rounded surface of the head than squares would be.

2. Glue head to the wooden block base with full-strength glue. Let dry.

3. Begin gluing newspaper triangles onto head with diluted white

*Fig. 14   The wig stand—"hair it is".*

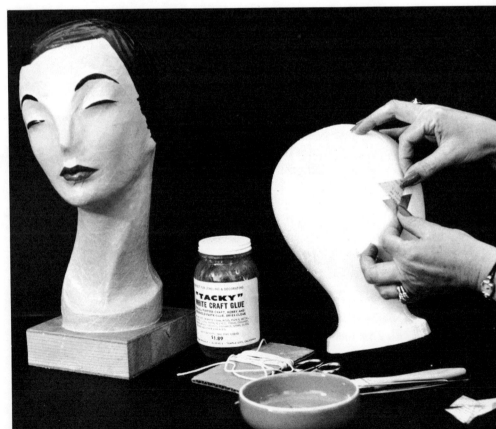

glue beginning at end of the nose (see figure 14). Go straight up the nose surface, gluing triangles pointing downward, each one over-lapping the former one. Continue in this way until entire head is covered. Create a smooth edge at the neck where it meets the stand, and cover wooden block with triangles also, if desired. Let dry.

4. When completely dry, paint head and stand with white titanium. Allow to dry.

5. Paint face and neck with flesh tone. Let dry.

6. To the flesh-tone paint add brown to get desired light brown or dark brown hair color. Or use yellow for blond, or choose any other hair coloring desired.

7. Paint features, using black to paint brows and eye line with .00 camel's hair artist's brush. Paint lips red.

8. Paint wooden base with contrasting color of acrylic paint, brown or black or use a color to match your room decor.

9. When all is well dried, give both head and base a coat of gloss varnish. Dry thoroughly before using.

10. Glue small circles of felt to four corners at bottom of base.

# 4.

## BOXES: RARE AND WONDERFUL

There is a special enchantment about a pretty box, whether it is a tiny one for trinkets, stamps or precious keepsakes or a larger one for handkerchiefs, gloves, sewing or other personal necessities. Too, a box is always a welcome gift for practically anyone from a child to a queen - or king!

Papier-mache boxes are wonderful to make. No two are alike and you can make them from discards in lovely, glowing colors or antique gold or silver, gem-encrusted for richly decorative, conversation-piece accessories or for luxurious utility.

Collect wooden, metal or plastic boxes. The base material should be sturdy enough to withstand the moisture from coatings of glue and paint. Although a cardboard cereal box was used as the lid for our first project, cardboard is not recommended for most articles because moisture may cause it to warp and twist out of shape. A very heavy pasteboard or composition-board box should work out fine.

### JEWELED TREASURE CHEST

Your friends will never believe this lovely jeweled chest for jewels, handkerchiefs or gloves was made of discards. It measures

10 ¾ inches in length, 6 inches wide and 6 inches to its domed top. It was made from a composition-board Oriental toy box and fitted with a round cereal box cut in half to make the domed lid.

## MATERIALS

> Composition-board box with hinged lid, approximately 6 by 11 inches
> Large round Quaker Oats cereal box, white glue
> Newspapers, heavy cord and lightweight cord
> Masking tape, small pans for glue and paint
> .00 camel's hair brush, 1-inch artist's brush
> Acrylic gloss varnish, acrylic paints: white titanium, marine blue, purple, black, green
> Gold paint, small brass hinges and hasp
> Clear lacquer spray
> Jewels, Bond cement

## METHOD

1. Remove hinged lid of the toy box. Using Basic Formula I instructions, cover bottom section of box with 1-inch newspaper squares over inside and outside and ½-inch squares for the inside. Using diluted white glue, glue the squares in even rows, also covering bottom of box. When finished, coat with glue and allow to dry thoroughly.

*Fig. 15 My treasured treasure chest (left) and two pretty boxes.* Made by Lura Smith.

Fig. 16 *The boxes are covered with newspaper squares.*

2. Paint with a coat of white titanium. Dry well.
3. Pencil on design or trace with carbon paper.
4. Split the round cereal box down the center. With masking tape fit the hollow half-cylinder to the toy box lid. Use plenty of tape,

Fig. 17 *Masking tape (see step 4 above) conceals the joining.*

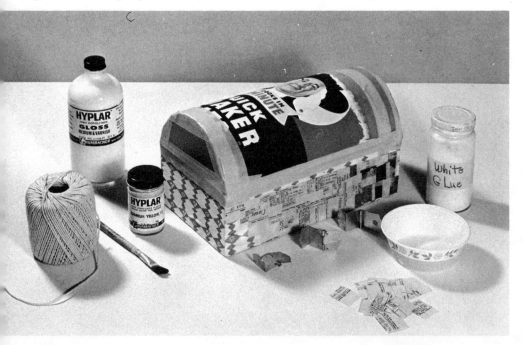

but make the joinings as flat and neat as possible so they will not show after painting (see figure 17).

5. Cover the entire lid with newspaper squares, gluing them both inside and out. Try not to saturate the dome top, since if it gets too wet it may warp when drying. When completely covered, coat with glue, and allow to dry.

6. Paint with white titanium, covering both inside and outside surface. Let dry.

7. A design of leaves and flowers can be drawn on or traced with carbon paper.

8. Apply cord to design (see figure 18). The cord used to outline the flowers and leaves is much finer than the heavy cord used to decorate the ends and side panels of the box. This gives a nice contrast, and also the finer cord is much easier to place on the more complicated pattern. Be sure to follow the basic directions for applying cord (Basic Formula I), using pre-shrunk twine and full-strength glue.

9. When cord is thoroughly dry, coat again with white titanium.

10. When this second white base coat is dry, paint the background

*Fig. 18    Cord saturated with full-strength glue is placed over the outlines in the "Treasure Chest" jewel box by Lura Smith.*

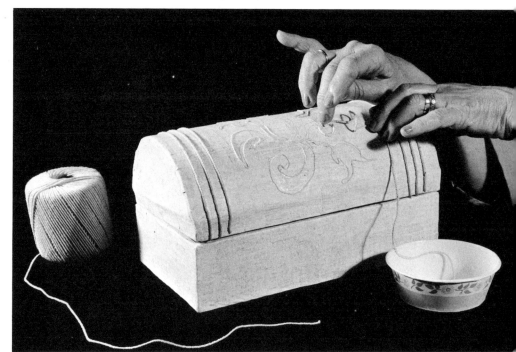

color and inside leaf and flower designs. This chest was painted inside and out with marine blue, flowers a deep purple, leaves green.
Carefully paint edges of cord where it is glued to the box surface so that no white will show.

11. Antique wash. Dilute black acrylic with water to make a thin wash. Brush over the entire chest, inside and out, wiping off with a soft cloth to give the antique effect.

12. When dry, paint cording with gold paint, using the small camel's hair brush.

13. When all paint is dry highlight with gold jeweler's paste rubbing the gold onto all cord outlines.

14. Coat entire box surface inside and out, including cord, with acrylic gloss varnish. Dry thoroughly.

15. Coat with clear lacquer spray.

16. Last of all, place the blue glass jewel "grape clusters" on the design if you are using the one in the illustration. These are sapphire blue, but if you have used another color for your box, you may wish to use other colors for the jewel "grapes." Use Bond cement to attach jewels.

17. Screw on the small brass hinges and hasp fittings to complete your Treasure Chest.

## TINY GOLD STAMP BOX

This little stamp box would be a delightful accessory for any lady's desk and, perhaps without the jewels on the lid, a welcome addition to a man's desk, too. It is 5 inches long, 2 inches wide and 1 inch high. Three wooden partitions inside provide "bins" for storing four different denominations of stamps.

### MATERIALS

Wooden craft box for stamps (found in hobby shops), or any hinged box of this size fitted with stamp compartments
Gold Oriental tea paper (found at import or Oriental stores)
Scissors, paste pan, Bond cement, white glue
Clear lacquer spray, acrylic gloss varnish
Gold paint, plastic jewels (gold and amethyst)

METHOD

1. Cut tea paper in tiny squares about ¼ inch wide and ½ to ¾ inch long.

2. Using diluted white glue, glue squares carefully, just to the edge of box sides and lid. Leave inside plain. Try not to get the gold paper too moist since the gold will run.

3. When thoroughly dry, cover gold-papered box with a coat of gloss varnish. Let dry.

4. Add coat of clear lacquer for seal coat.

5. When lacquer is completely dry place jewels with Bond cement in a pleasing design on lid of box (see figure 15). Another design is an elongated "S" made of jewels down the center length of lid using four amethyst plastic jewels for the top and bottom loops of the "S," placing a gold jewel in the center and two gold tear-drop jewels or cabochons for accent. The "S" can mean "Stamps," or, if you wish, a monogram letter could be used. Use jewels to match your study or den, or, if the box is to be for a man's desk, a small metallic heraldic emblem or animal, or a metal initial.

## ANTIQUE GOLD BOX

This lovely box for trinkets was made from a hinged wooden box measuring 5 by 4½ inches. The inside was painted turquoise

*Fig. 19    Antique gold box with a gold cord vine trailing down the sides.* Author's collection.

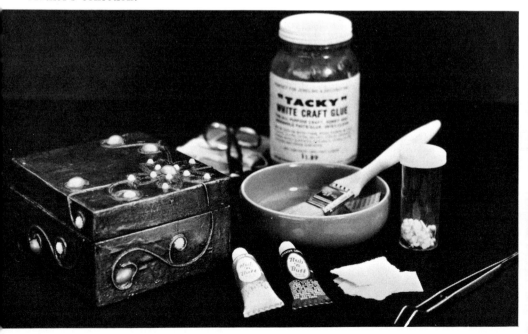

blue to contrast with the antique gold effect of the outer surfaces. Turquoise and white plastic cabochons and beads decorate it in a graceful vine outlined with fine gold cord. A lace medallion was also used in the design.

## MATERIALS

> Hinged wooden box, clean newspapers
> White glue, fine chalk-line cord
> Acrylic paints: white titanium, turquoise, gloss varnish, black, burnt umber
> Gold spray paint or Chromotone
> Paint brushes—1-inch and .00
> Lace medallion, white and turquoise cabochons (jewels, plastic)
> Resin or clear lacquer coating

## METHOD

1. Tear newspaper evenly into pieces measuring approximately 2½ inches by 2 and 3 inches. Paper towels would give quite an interesting rough texture if you wish to try something different. The rather large squares are placed in a helter-skelter arrangement on the box, and this, too, adds interest.

2. Using diluted white glue as in Basic Method I, completely cover both inside and outside of box with squares. After it's entirely covered, coat with remaining diluted glue and let dry.

3. When thoroughly dry, paint box inside and out with white titanium and allow to dry. When dry, paint inside of box with turquoise.

4. Pencil on design. The lace flower medallion is placed on the left front corner of the lid, and the lines for cording are drawn to resemble a vine with tendrils which curl around the jewels. Extend the tendrils over the edge of the lid and draw the vine as if it were continuing on over the sides of the box (see figure 19).

5. Glue the lace medallion onto the box top with full-strength white glue, then saturate preshrunk cord with full-strength glue and apply over pattern lines. Allow to dry thoroughly.

6. Give entire box including cord and medallion a coat of white titanium acrylic. Allow to dry.

7. Now paint the outside of box and lid with gold spray paint or Chromotone. Also paint the inside edges of both lid and bottom with gold.

8. When all has thoroughly dried, make a wash using burnt umber acrylic mixed with water, following directions in Basic Method I, and antique the entire outside surfaces of box and lid. Allow to dry.

9. Coat with gloss varnish inside and out.

10. When dry, give a coat of resin or clear lacquer spray.

11. When dry, place plastic jewels in vine tendrils with Bond cement.

*Note:* Be very careful throughout that no paint gets on the hinges.

## SILVER TRINKET BOX

This little trinket box is clever and colorful, trimmed with silver cord in a six-point star design and bedecked with green and blue tear-drop jewels. The inside is finished in marine blue.

MATERIALS

    Hinged wooden box 4¼ by 2¼ inches high—this may be an old one you have, or a craft box purchased at an art supply or hobby shop

    Newspaper squares from about ½ to ¾ inch

    Oriental tea paper in fancy design, or metallic paper like that in Christmas cards and envelope linings and, sometimes in wallpaper

    White glue, medium cord

    Acrylic paints: marine blue, white titanium, gloss varnish

    Silver paint, silver-blue jeweler's paste

    Blue and green tear-drop plastic jewels, Bond cement

    Clear lacquer spray

METHOD

1. Following Basic Method I, mix diluted white glue, and cover box with newspaper squares inside and out. Coat with remaining glue and allow to dry thoroughly.

2. Paint with white titanium and allow to dry.

3. Plan and draw design on box lid. Draw a small circle in center of lid (a round plastic jewel will be glued on this later). Draw lines out from the circle to make a six-pointed star. On the sides of the box draw large pointed scallops, two to a side.

4. Paint cord with marine blue and hang up to dry or lay on wax paper.

5. Cut six starpoint sections to fit design. Glue in place with

full-strength white glue. An art cardboard with mottled colors of green, blue, silver and gold was used here.

6. Glue painted cord when dry to design outlines, scallops and star with full-strength glue. Let dry.

7. Paint box inside and out with marine blue. Let dry.

8. Make an antique wash (see Basic Method I) using black acrylic, and antique entire outside of box. Dry.

9. Paint cord with silver paint. When dry, highlight cord and box with silver-blue jeweler's paste.

10. When all is dry, give box a coat of gloss varnish.

11. When box is dry, use Bond cement to glue on green and blue plastic tear-drop cabochons alternately between star points. Use a round blue cabochon for the center. Place green and blue tear-drops alternately in scallop points on the sides.

## OCTAGONAL SEWING BOX

This octagonal wooden box was already fitted with hinges and a hasp for locking. One similar to it should be easy to find. If it's to be used for valuables, a tiny gold padlock would be practical. It is large enough for important papers as it measures 12 by 12 inches and is 3 inches deep. The flower design is in shades of orange, red and yellow with a background of russet.

MATERIALS

> Octagonal box, white glue
> Newspaper squares cut to 1½-inch size
> Fine pre-shrunk cord, paint brushes
> Acrylic paints: white titanium, orange, red, yellow, green, russet, gloss varnish
> Gold paint, clear lacquer
> Yellow stamens, plastic jewel

METHOD

1. Following Basic Method I, glue newspaper squares with diluted white glue both inside and outside of lid, leaving the lip edge uncovered. Beginning at edges of sides of both box and lid, glue squares on in straight, even rows, remembering to overlap squares. Coat with remainder of diluted glue and allow to dry.

2. Paint with white titanium acrylic. Let dry.

3. Trace on flower and leaf design. This one (see figure 20) is reminiscent of a dahlia, with several rows of petals done in different colors. The leaves surround the flower on short, curving stems.

4. Using full-strength glue place pre-shrunk cord on design, pressing firmly. You will find that fine cord will be easier to use with a complicated design such as the one shown than thick or heavy cord.

5. When cord is thoroughly dry, paint over entire box, including cord with white titanium acrylic. Let dry thoroughly.

6. Paint entire box including the inside of lid with russet or whatever color you choose for the background. Use a light tint of orange for the box inside.

7. Paint flower design inside cord outlines. Be sure to paint edges of cord next to lid so no white areas will show. The center

*Fig. 20  Flower and leaf design on octagonal sewing box.* Made by Lura Smith.

row of petals are red, the second row yellow, the third orange and the outside row is red. Leaves are a medium green and a chartreuse green. Dry thoroughly before antiquing.

8. Make antique wash with either black or burnt sienna thinned with water (directions in Basic Method I). Brush over entire box, including painted flower design. Wipe off carefully with soft cloth to give antique effect.

9. When completely dry, paint cord with gold paint or rub gold jeweler's paste on with fingers.

10. Give one coat of gloss varnish over cord, design and entire box inside and outside. Dry thoroughly.

11. Add one coat clear lacquer. Dry well.

12. Use Bond cement to glue short stamens to center of flower design. Also glue a yellow cabochon jewel to center.

## CIGAR BOX TREASURES

The next three projects (see figure 21) are simple, beautiful and useful boxes made from wooden cigar boxes. The first has a marvelous textured surface, the second shimmers like antique gold, the third has a heavy bark-like finish.

### *PLATINUM JEWEL BOX

> Hinged wooden cigar box
> Grumbacher's Modeling Paste or similar substance
> Wax paper, white glue
> Black acrylic paint
> Silver jeweler's paste, purple velour crepe paper

METHOD

1. Using a sheet of wax paper to work on, apply modeling paste with fingers or a spatula to the outside surface of box lid, covering only to the outside edges. Work in any texture design you wish. The one illustrated was done in an interesting swirl pattern with the fingers. Be careful to keep paste off of hinges and the closing edges of the box.

2. Cover bottom and sides of box in the same way, forming four small legs with the paste at the four corners of the bottom. Allow to dry thoroughly, two or three days, depending on thickness of the paste layer.

*Fig. 21   Treasure boxes created from ordinary cigar boxes.*

3. When well dried, paint the entire box with black paint, covering paste layer and edges of lid and box which have been left uncovered.

4. When paint is dry, accent higher surfaces of design with silver jeweler's paste. Let dry half an hour to an hour, then buff with soft cloth.

5. Cut velour paper to size and glue to the inside surfaces of both lid and box, using a very firm white glue (one that is not too moist). Use glue sparingly or it will show through the paper.

6. Fasten a metal hasp for a tiny gold padlock to front of box if you like.

## GOLD HANDKERCHIEF BOX

### MATERIALS

Wooden cigar box
Gold Oriental tea paper
Joli Glaze clear lacquer spray; white glue
1-inch brush
Metal hasp
Red velour ribbon, very wide, or velour crepe paper
Acrylic paints: black, burnt umber

METHOD

1. Make a very thin antique wash with burnt umber paint and a small amount of black. (See Basic Method I.) Antique the sheet of gold Oriental tea paper with the brown wash. The gold color will run a little bit, but this adds to the antique look. Allow to dry.

2. Cut the tea paper into 1½-inch squares.

3. Using diluted glue, place squares over top and side surfaces of the box, leaving inside edges of top and bottom uncovered (closing edges). Trim the squares to fit neatly around box hinges (if lid is hinged) and do not get glue on them.

4. When lid is dry, cover bottom part of box. Allow to dry thoroughly.

5. Brush on a coat of clear lacquer (Joli Glaze is recommended specifically for this box). Lacquer the closing edges of box with the glaze. When lid is dry, glaze bottom part of box, applying glaze over the hinges and hasp. Move lid up and down to keep hinges from sticking in one position. The glaze will keep the metal from discoloring.

6. Cut velour ribbon or paper to size and glue lining with thick full-strength glue (not moist) to inside of box and lid. Use glue sparingly.

7. Attach metal hasp if desired.


GIFT BOX

A beautiful handkerchief, curio, or gift box decorated with a handpainted picture on bark made by children outside of Guadalajara, Mexico.

MATERIALS

> Cigar box with hinged lid
> Gold paint, medium weight cord, white glue
> Heavy-duty commercial paper towels
> Velour cloth or felt lining
> Picture: the one shown is painted on bark and may be obtained in art shops (see Glossary, Art Enterprizes). Or use any picture you wish; even a Christmas card if it is large enough
> Wallpaper paste, wax paper
> Acrylic paints: Mars black, matte varnish

METHOD

1. Cut heavy paper towels in ¾-inch squares.

2. Glue with diluted white glue, beginning at edge of lid. Glue squares all the way around the sides and top, extending part of the way under picture area. Overlap squares a tiny fraction, keeping them even.

3. After lid is covered, begin gluing squares at top edge of box sides, taking care to glue in a very straight line along top edge, keeping squares even, then doing second row, etc., until box is covered. Dry thoroughly.

4. When dry, turn box over and glue squares to bottom. Dry.

5. Place box on wax paper and glue preshrunk cord around base of box with full-strength glue. Place another length of cord around top edge of lid.

6. Glue picture to center top. If using a picture that is fairly thick use wallpaper paste to be sure it will lie flat.

7. Paint length of cord to be used around picture with gold paint and dry before gluing around picture.

8. While cord is drying, paint box and glued-on cord with white titanium, being careful not to get any on picture.

9. When dry, glue gold cord around picture, using full-strength glue.

10. Paint entire box with gold paint. Dry.

11. Antique wash: make thin wash with Mars black. Brush over entire box, but not picture. Dry well.

12. Give box, including picture and cord, two coats of matte varnish, drying well between coats.

13. Line inside of box with any color velour cloth or felt.

## *EAGLE FILE BOX

I'll bet any man would like this box with its patriotic golden-eagle decoration for his desk or bureau. It makes a handy place to store collections of small articles.

MATERIALS

Wooden craft box, or one glued together from scraps, 8 by 4½ by 4 inches
Heavyweight pre-shrunk cord, white glue

Newspaper cut in 1½-inch squares
Acrylic paints: black, white titanium, gloss varnish
Gold spray paint, gold jeweler's paste
Gold (Venus Bronzing) powder, turpentine

METHOD

1. Spray paint inside of box with gold, also box lid.

2. When gold paint is dry, glue newspaper squares neatly over the outer surface of box and lid using diluted glue (read directions for Basic Method I at beginning of book). Do not cover closing edges of lid and box or the bottom. If the box is hinged, do not get glue on the hinges; cut the squares carefully to fit around them. If you want to make a hinge that will let the lid open, see next step. If not, go on to step 4.

3. You can make a hinge for the lid by gluing a strip of cotton twill, used for sewing, across the back of the box and back of lid, using full-strength white glue. Then glue the newspaper squares just up to the place where the lid will bend when opened. Paint the squares with plenty of diluted glue and open the lid several times while the cotton strip is drying and if it pulls away, more glue can be added to the cotton strip.

4. When box and lid are completely covered, paint with the remainder of the diluted glue, pushing down with your fingers any squares that may be trying to pop up, then set on a piece of wax paper and allow to dry thoroughly.

5. When box is dried, paint with white titanium. Allow to dry.

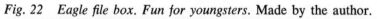

*Fig. 22   Eagle file box. Fun for youngsters.* Made by the author.

6. Trace an eagle design on the box lid with carbon paper, or draw one like the illustration. Outline the sides and top of box in panels, using a ruler. The eagle is a simple design to draw freehand. Draw straight lines for the wings at the top and curving lines for the lower areas. Do not make the lines too short or with sharp corners, except at the eagle's beak which can be the starting edge of your cord.

7. Using full-strength glue, run the lengths of preshrunk cord through your fingers to saturate it, then press over the lines you have drawn on the box. If you do not use preshrunk cord (see Basic Method I for directions) the cord will shrink as it dries and your design will warp out of shape.

8. When cord is all glued on, let dry thoroughly, then paint with a second coat of white titanium, painting the cord also. Let dry.

9. Now paint the box with black, painting the bottom edges of the cord where it is glued to the box, but not inside the eagle design. Let dry.

10. Paint cord and inside eagle design with gold paint. You may buy the paint already mixed, or mix gold powder with Bronzing Liquid. Do not make too much at a time because it goes a long way.

11. When the cord and eagle design have dried thoroughly, make a wash using a small amount of gold powder and quite a lot of turpentine, so that it is a thin gold liquid (very thin). Paint this gold wash over the black surfaces lightly. The wash will separate as it dries, giving the box a decidedly antique effect.

12. When box is dry, you can highlight the cord with gold jeweler's paste if you wish.

13. Paint entire box, even the eagle design, with acrylic gloss varnish.

14. When dry, coat with clear lacquer spray or glaze.

15. Apply metal hinges and hasp if desired.

# 5.

## GLAMOUR JEWELRY FROM
## PAPER BAGS

No one will ever guess that these are made from ordinary brown paper grocery bags and odds and ends of cardboard! They are practical since they are almost unbreakable, and excitingly different, looking like the most fragile porcelain. Make some to accessorize a costume and you will be thought of as "that clever person who makes her own jewelry".

### PINK AND GOLD FLOWER PIN

The daintiest pink and gold Dresden-like blossom pin. You will astonish your friends when you wear this or give it as a gift.

#### MATERIALS

Brown paper grocery bag, white glue
Gesso, Gook, gold-color pin back
Aluminum foil, wax paper
Acrylic paints: white titanium, pink, black, matte varnish
Gold jeweler's paste
Camel's hair brush, size .00
Large pink, faceted jewel
Pink pearls, Bond cement

METHOD

1. Cut two identical flower shapes from heavy brown paper grocery bag (see illustration). This pin, shown in color, has heart-shaped petals. Cut two more flower shapes slightly smaller than the first two for the inside set of petals. Be sure the larger ones are exactly the size you want for your pin because it is easy to get it too large.

2. Mix diluted white glue and pour into shallow bowl. Soak one paper flower in the glue until it is saturated. Remove from glue and place over its matching paper cutout. Shape the double paper flower with fingers, curling petals into the desired shape and position (check with illustration).

3. Crush a piece of aluminum foil around and under the flower petals so it will prop up and hold the flower in position while drying. Repeat with the second set of petals.

4. When larger set of petals is thoroughly dry, glue on the gold-colored pin back (finding) with Bond cement to back of flower, slightly above center. Cover metal shank with a piece of masking tape.

5. Brush at least four coats of Gesso (see Glossary) on back and front of petals, covering masking tape on back, also. Allow to dry thoroughly between coats. The Gesso will build up the china-like surface of the pin. Be sure the Gesso is not too thick for it will leave brush marks on the surface. Thin with water if necessary. Place on wax paper to dry between coatings.

6. When both sets of petals have been built up to your satisfaction and are well dried, edge the outer border of each with Gook directly from the tube. Let dry.

7. Paint both sets of petals with one coat of white titanium. Dry.

8. Paint with pink (or use any color you prefer). Let dry.

9. Place a drop of full-strength white glue into center front of larger petal (which will be the back of pin). Place smaller flower inside larger, pressing down firmly on glue. Alternate petals so that one will not be on top of the other (see color plate).

10. Dip camel's hair artist's brush into black and wipe off excess. Shade in brush strokes from the center of flower to edges very lightly, giving a "dry brush" effect.

11. Highlight the raised borders with gold jeweler's paste, also touch the petals with a suggestion of the gold.

12. Coat the entire pin with matte varnish and allow to dry on wax paper.

13. Using Bond cement, glue a large pink glass faceted jewel in the center of flower pin and surround it with a circle of small pink pearls. (Or, if using other colors, harmonize the jewel colors.)

The next project shows how to make earrings to match the pin.

## PINK AND GOLD FLOWER EARRINGS

These are illustrated with the flower pin in color. They are made exactly the same as the flower pin with these exceptions:

1. Cut much smaller petals, placing them up to your ear to see exactly what size you wish. The earrings will be single, not double like the pin, unless you prefer to make double ones.

2. Three small pink pearls are glued in the center of the finished earrings.

3. Using Bond cement, glue earring backs to petal backs, making sure to use gold colored ones to match the pin finding. Do not attach earring backs until flower petals are completely finished.

## BLUE AND SILVER FLOWER PIN

This lovely pin looks like a pansy although it is not an exact copy of any real flower.

MATERIALS

Brown paper grocery bag, white glue
Gesso, Gook, aluminum foil, wax paper
Camel's hair brush, size .00
Silver jeweler's paste
Sapphire blue faceted glass rhinestone, small oval faceted glass jewels of darker blue, small white pearls
Silver pin back finding
Acrylic paints: white titanium, blue, matte varnish
Silver paint
Bond cement

METHOD

1. Cut two identical flower shapes from brown paper (see figure 23). Be careful to get the exact size you want for your pin. Do not cut them too large.

2. Pour diluted glue into shallow bowl and soak one paper flower until saturated. Remove from glue and place it over matching cutout. Shape with fingers, curling petals into the desired shape and position as it dries on wax paper.

3. When dry, glue silver pin backing a little above center back using Bond cement.

4. Brush front and back of flower with three coats of Gesso or Modeling paste and Extender (see index). Give three coats, allowing it to dry between each coat. Paint over the metal shank of the pin (be careful not to get any on the pin hinge), building up over the shank so it becomes part of the pin. Or cover shank with masking tape, and cover with Gesso.

5. When flower is dry, outline the outer border of flower with Gook (as in illustration) to add a raised edge for the silver decoration. Dry.

6. Paint with one coat of white titanium. Let dry.

7. Paint with blue paint (or use any color you wish). Dry.

8. Dip clean camel's hair brush into silver paint, wiping off ex-

*Fig. 23 In preparation: blue and silver flower pin and earrings.* Made by Lura Smith.

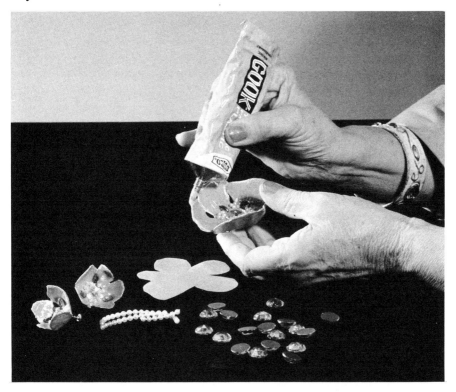

cess. Draw brush from center of flower to outside edges of each petal. Paint raised Gook borders with silver.

9. When dry, highlight petals and edges with silver jeweler's paste if you would like a richer silver decoration.

10. Coat with matte varnish over complete surface of pin. Dry well.

11. Use full-strength white glue or Bond cement to glue a large blue faceted glass jewel in center of pin. Glue alternate oval glass jewels and pearls around center jewel.

The next project gives matching earrings.

## BLUE AND SILVER EARRINGS

Follow the steps for the pin given above, but cut the flower the exact size you wish for your earrings. They will be much smaller than the pin, of course (see illustration).

Instead of the pin finding, glue finished flowers to silver earring backs, placing them a little above center so they will not droop when you wear them.

## FLOWER HEADBAND

Set off your tresses with a fashionable flower headband. This one is made in blue and silver of simple paper blossoms but they are as hard and firm as porcelain.

MATERIALS

> Plastic hair band, white glue
> Brown paper grocery bag, shallow bowl
> Gesso, Gook, or modeling paste and extender
> Aluminum foil, wax paper, camel's hair brush, size .00
> Acrylic paints: blue or other color, white titanium
> Acrylic gloss or matte varnish
> 24-gauge wire
> Tiny silver, gold or colored beads
> Silver or gold jeweler's paste

METHOD

1. Cut seven small, five-petalled single flowers from brown paper bag, all the same size. (See figure 24.)

*Fig. 24 These porcelain-like hair-ornaments are made of paper, of course.*
By Lura Smith.

2. Mix diluted white glue in shallow bowl. Soak each flower in the glue until paper is saturated. Remove and shape with fingers, laying it to dry on wax paper or crushed aluminum foil, continuing to pinch into shape as flowers are drying.

3. Push a wire through center of flower to facilitate handling and when completely dry paint with four coats of Gesso or modeling paste, thinning if necessary, drying well between coats. Hang to dry or place on wax paper.

4. When dry, outline edges of flowers with a very tiny border of Gook. Dry well before painting.

5. Paint all flowers with white titanium. Dry well.

6. Paint with blue or color you choose. Dry.

7. Rub silver or gold jeweler's paste on raised borders with finger. Also rub a tiny bit on flower petals to accent them.

8. Apply a coat of gloss or matte varnish, whichever you prefer. The gloss varnish will give a shiny finish, the matte a duller one. Let dry.

9. Place a drop of full-strength white glue into center of flower and drop tiny silver or gold beads (matching color of the jeweler's paste you have used) onto the blob of glue. Let dry.

10. Attach flowers to plastic headband with wire already in flower. Twist wire to secure flower firmly and snip off excess.

## BLOSSOM HAIRPIN

Pretty and exotic, this hair adornment can be made at the same time as the headband.

### MATERIALS

Same as for Flower Headband (above) with the exception of the large metal or plastic hairpin

### METHOD

Proceed as for flower headband (above), but cut only one flower for each hairpin. When flower is dry and the beads have been glued into the center, attach with wire to the hairpin.

## LIME GREEN AND BLACK PIN

This decorative pin (figure 25) is truly different. It is indestructible, remains pliable, and is perfectly beautiful on a suit.

### MATERIALS

Paper bag, newspaper squares
White glue, cord, cleansing tissue
Pin back finding, small glass
Acrylic paint: lime green, black, gloss varnish
Gold jeweler's paste

### METHOD

1. Cut two identical flower patterns from paper bag (see figure 25).
2. Mix diluted white glue in shallow bowl. Dip and glue flowers together, bending petals back to shape flower.
3. Place flower in the top of a small glass to dry, but keep shaping and bending down the tips of petals while drying.
4. When dry, glue pin back finding to back of flower, placing it a little above center. Use full-strength glue.

*I.* Above: *angel wall tableau, page 145. II.* Left: *large decorator candleholder, page 135. III. little owl, page 113. IV. red apple salad bowl, page 111.*

*V.* Below: *Christmas ideas. Right to left—Nut topiary tree, page 130; crescent holly swag, page 128; poinsettia goblet candleholder, page 142; decorator compote, page 134.*

VI. Left: *Tissue box cover, page 23; pixie spray can cover, page 25; wastebasket, page 20. VII. Below: Pink and gold pin and earrings, pages 58-60; bracelets, pages 70-89.*

5. Cut newspaper squares ¼-inch size and glue with diluted mixture to back of pin, covering the base of the metal finding also. If the squares extend over edges, do not try trimming them while wet. When they are dry, you can easily cut them off with scissors. The newspaper gives the pin strength and helps retain its shape. Let dry.

6. When pin has dried, dip ¼ of a square of cleansing tissue into the diluted glue, wad it up and squeeze out excess. Place this in the center of the flower, patting it down well.

7. Cut cord into 1½-inch and 2-inch lengths. Use full-strength white glue and place two short lengths and a longer one in the center on each petal. Have cord ends almost touching center of flower and radiating outward as in illustration.

8. When cord and tissue are well dried, paint entire flower with lime green. Let dry.

9. Make an antique wash with black (see Basic Method I). Apply the wash heavily to the center of flower and outer edges of each petal. With brush or your finger, smear a little of the wash over the remaining green of petals, wiping off nearly all of the black, leaving just enough to tone down the color. Apply the wash to back of pin also.

10. When dry, highlight the dark center and cord with gold jeweler's paste.

*Fig. 25    Lime green pin (back row, left and right); pattern (front row left). Morning glory pin and Coral Gardenia pin in center; 5-petal pattern for gardenia at right.*

11. Give entire pin three coats of gloss or matte varnish, depending on finish desired, drying well between coats.

*Note*: The pin at the far right in the illustration is made in the same way as this project, with the exception of coiled, glued cord instead of tissue for the center. Radiating cord is also omitted.

## MORNING GLORY PIN

Make a lovely pin like the one shown in figure 16 and it will bloom forever on summery print and pastel frocks. Ours was done in orange, but the morning glory flowers in blue, yellow, rose and scarlet too.

### MATERIALS

> Instant Papier-Mache Mix (see Basic Method III)
> Or homemade papier-mache (see Basic Method II)
> Bowl, wooden spoon, white glue
> Plastic flower for mold
> Acrylic paints: white titanium, orange, gloss or matte varnish
> Gesso, camel's hair brush, wax paper, plastic bag
> Stamens, pin back finding

*Fig. 26    A plastic flower is the mold; instant mix is applied to its back.*

METHOD

1. Choose flat plastic flower similar to illustration to use as a mold. Remove it from stem and leaves which will not be used. Notice that the back of the plastic flower petals are more deeply veined than the inside surfaces. The papier-mache mixture will therefore be placed on the *back* of the plastic flower petals.

2. Prepare papier-mache mixture. About one-half cup will be needed for one pin. If you make more than this, it can be kept in the refrigerator in a plastic bag. The ready-made mix can also be prepared in a plastic bag.

3. Working on a piece of wax paper, pat the wet mix about ½-inch thick onto the back of the plastic petals. (See figure 26.) Smooth the pulp from the center to the edge, smoothing edges as neatly as possible. The edges can be a little thinner than the inner portions of petals. Allow to dry overnight or a day or two at room temperature until hard and completely dry. Time will depend on the amount of moisture used in the mix and also on the weather humidity and temperature. *Note*: If you wish it to dry faster, place on a cookie sheet or aluminum foil and place in a 140-degree oven, *leaving the door open*. It will dry in several hours, but do not turn the oven any higher than 140 degrees or the papier-mache will crack and warp out of shape.

4. When thoroughly dry the papier-mache can be popped out of the plastic mold. Remove carefully, but if it should tear, it can be easily mended with more wet mixture.

5. Glue the metal pin backing to flower back and cover the shank with a small amount of the papier-mache mix, smoothing and making it blend into the flower back.

6. Apply Gesso which has been thinned with water to the consistency of thick cream. Give front and back of pin several coatings, drying well between coats.

7. Mix white titanium and orange paints together to get shade you wish. Paint entire pin, front and back, taking care not to get paint on pin hinge or safety clasp, if it has one.

8. When nearly dry, use white titanium and an almost dry brush to shade from center of flower to about 1-inch radius, giving a delicate shaded effect.

9. When dry, give several coats of gloss or matte varnish. Glue stamens in center with full-strength glue.

## CORAL GARDENIA PIN

Although this pin is made of cardboard, it looks like delicate Dresden china.  It is outstanding—almost like wearing a corsage!

### MATERIALS

Cardboard from a tablet back
White glue, Gesso, artist's brush
Acrylic paints: white titanium, yellow, red, pearl essence, gloss varnish
Wax paper
Metal pin back, pearl stamens

### METHOD

1. Cut a six-petalled flower from the cardboard, similar to the illustration.  Be careful to cut the exact size you wish.  Cut a smaller five-petalled flower to match.

2. Dilute white glue as in instructions for Basic Method I, pour in a shallow bowl and soak both flower shapes in the glue until they are saturated and pliable.

3. Remove flower form and shape while wet, working on wax paper, curving and pinching the separate petals as in illustration. Continue pinching and forcing the damp cardboard to retain its shape as it dries.  Dry on clean sheet of wax paper.

4. When dry, glue the metal pin backing a little above center back of large petals, using full-strength glue.

5. Thin Gesso with water, if necessary, so that no brush strokes will show.  Apply several coats to both sets of petals, covering the metal pin shank also, but be careful not to get any Gesso or paint on the hinges or catch.  Five or six coats will not be too much; build up the edges of the petals also, to give them a rounded, smooth finish.  Dry well between coats.

6. When you have the "china" effect you wish and the petals are completely dry, paint with a mixture of yellow and red acrylic, if you wish the coral shade, mixing with white titanium to soften the color.  Dry well.

7. Glue the small flower section inside the large one, using full-strength glue.  Alternate petals to add interest.

8. Add five drops of pearl essence to about one ounce of gloss varnish and paint entire pin. Dry well.

9. Glue several clusters of the pearl stamens in the center of your gardenia with full-strength glue or Bond cement.

## FLOWER PIN

This is made in exactly the same manner as the Lime Green and Black Pin but with the different treatment of the flower center. The cord is coiled and glued into the center with full-strength white glue.

# 6.

## FANTASTIC BRACELETS FROM BLEACH BOTTLES

Light and lovely boutique bracelets made from bleach bottles and cardboard tubes? You have to see these to believe it! You can wear them from elbow to wrist, match them to every outfit. We have seen bracelets not half as pretty at jewelry counters in fine stores. (See figure 27.)

*Fig. 27   Bleach bottle bracelets: back row (left to right), A, B, C, D; front row, E, F; all are described in the text.*

## A - BLUE AND WHITE WITH SILVER

MATERIALS

    Plastic bleach bottle, sharp scissors
    Stapler, newspaper, white glue
    Masking tape, cord, Bond cement
    Acrylic paints: white titanium, blue, black, gloss varnish
    Silver Venus Bronzing Powder, turpentine
    Silver jeweler's paste
    Clear lacquer spray
    White beads, blue rhinestones, flat-sided pearls
    Ruler, pencil, wax paper
    Artist's paint brushes

BASIC METHOD FOR ALL BLEACH BOTTLE BRACELETS

1. Cut off the top of bleach bottle just below handle, then cut off bottom. When you cut and flatten out the plastic cylinder you will find that you have a straight rectangular sheet to use for bracelets.

2. Measure a strip one-inch wide and draw a line the long way of the plastic sheet. Cut with scissors, or use an X-Acto knife or razor.

3. Double your hand into as small a fist as you can, fit plastic strip around it and cut the strip to this length. This gives you your own personal bracelet size.

*Fig. 28   Materials used for bracelets showing bleach bottle strip, cardboard tubes and plastic ring (4 center rings).*

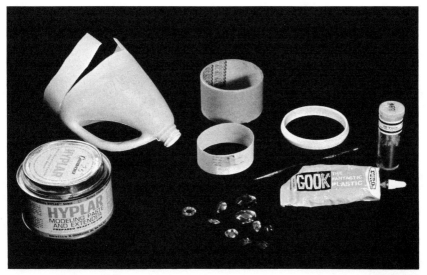

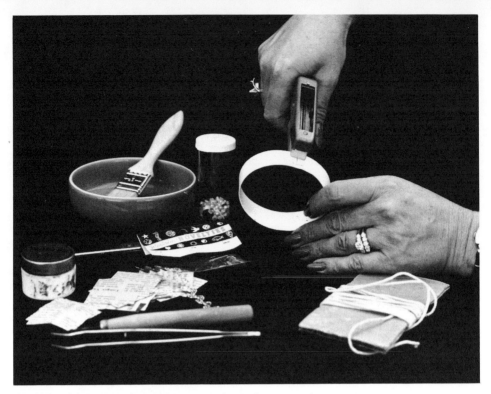

*Fig. 29   Staple plastic bottle strip across the cut ends.*

*Fig. 30   Fringe the tape as described in step 5.*

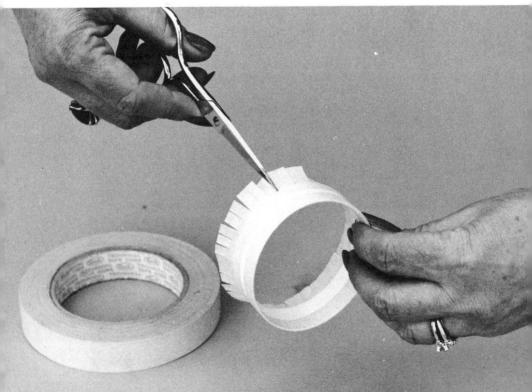

4. Place ends of strip together so that the edges are butting, and staple three times *across* the cut ends (see figure 29). Cover staples with masking tape on both inside and outside of bracelet.

5. Cover edges of bracelet with masking tape, allowing half the tape strip to jut above the bracelet edge. Fringe the tape down to the plastic and fold to inside (see figure 30). Be sure edges are very smooth, with no wrinkles. Cover both edges.

6. Mix diluted white glue (see Basic Formula I). Cut newspaper into ¼-inch squares and glue inside bracelet, neatly covering masking tape, overlapping squares from edge to edge. It is easier to do this by working with a small paint brush, picking up the squares and placing on the bracelet surface which has been coated with glue. Or you may cover the inside surface of bracelet with masking tape, taking care that it does not stick out over the edges.

7. Use ¼-inch newspaper squares on the outside surface of bracelet for a truly antique effect, making sure all is covered to edge of bracelet. Do not fold the squares over the edges of bracelet, but glue them to the exact edges. Masking tape can be used to cover the outside instead of using the squares, but is not half as pretty. Still, if you are in a hurry, you can try it.

8. When both inside and outside surfaces are neatly covered, coat with the diluted glue and allow to dry thoroughly on a piece of wax, paper.

9. Cut two lengths of preshrunk cord a little longer than it takes to go completely around bracelet. Glue to both edges with full-strength white glue, pressing cord down firmly. When ends meet, trim with scissors and twist together neatly. Let dry, then glue another length of cord in the center in a scalloped or curving design. Let dry.

10. When thoroughly dry, paint with white titanium, covering inside and outside surfaces and cord. Let dry on wax paper.

11. Paint with light blue, again covering the entire bracelet, including cord. Dry.

12. Make a thin silver antique wash using the silver powder and turpentine. Brush this wash thinly over bracelet, leaving the inside of bracelet plain if you wish. Dry well.

13. Highlight cord either by painting with silver paint or rubbing with silver jeweler's paste.

14. Apply a coat of gloss varnish over the entire bracelet. Let dry thoroughly.

15. Give one coat of clear lacquer spray. Dry.

16. Use Bond cement to glue white beads and blue glass jewels in various patterns inside loops or beside curves of cord. When glue has set, your bracelet is ready to wear.

*Note:* This basic method can be varied to make many styles. Gook or modeling paste can be used for decoration instead of cord. Apply glass and plastic jewels, glass blobs, metallic braid, odds and ends of beads, and many other objects in wild and wonderful designs of your own. Run the gamut of colors, and make earrings to match for wonderful gift sets.

## B - BLACK AND GOLD

### MATERIALS

The materials are almost the same as for Project A with these exceptions:

Gold jeweler's paste, green and amber glass jewels
Gold Japanese tea paper

### METHOD

1. Cut a 1½-inch strip of bleach bottle plastic.

2. Measure over doubled fist and staple across the two joining ends. (*Note:* Never overlap these.) Cover staples with masking tape lapped around inside and outside over joining.

3. Bind edges with masking tape as explained in Project A.

4. Cut gold Japanese tea paper into small ¼-inch to ½-inch squares. Glue with diluted white glue to bracelet band inside and out, overlapping squares a tiny fraction, but gluing only to the edges—do not turn over edge. Dry thoroughly. Glue two rows of cord around edges. Dry.

5. Make a medium thin black wash. Antique inside and outside surfaces of bracelet, wiping off excess with soft cloth, covering cord also. This bracelet should look black with the gold showing through.

6. When dry, highlight cord with gold jeweler's paste.

7. Give entire bracelet a coat of gloss varnish. Dry.

8. Give one coat of clear lacquer. Dry.

9. Use Bond cement to glue oval-shaped, faceted glass green and amber jewels in an interesting pattern around bracelet.

## C - GOLD WITH RED AND AMBER STONES

An outstandingly beautiful bracelet. It is also illustrated in color.

MATERIALS

Same as in Project A with these additions:
Gold Japanese tea paper, gold paint

METHOD

1. After stapling band and covering edges with masking tape as in the basic method for Project A, this chapter, glue squares of gold tea paper to outside of band, overlapping squares in rows from edge to edge. Use diluted glue. Let dry.
2. Line inside surface with masking tape.
3. Use full-strength white glue to place preshrunk cord around bracelet edges. Allow to dry.
4. Paint masking tape lining with white titanium. Let dry.
5. Mix gold paint, using Bronzing Powder and Medium. Paint cord. Let dry.
6. Make a wash with remaining paint mixed with turpentine. Antique inside surface of bracelet. Dry.
7. Brush entire bracelet with gloss varnish. Dry well.
8. Give a coat of clear lacquer spray or Joli Glaze (a liquid resin product which gives a very hard, shiny surface).
9. When bracelet is thoroughly dry, glue jewels with Bond cement. The square red glass jewels, alternating with amber oval-shaped jewels set in an interesting pattern around the bracelet, lend much to its attractiveness.

## D - PINK AND GOLD SLAVE BRACELET

MATERIALS

Same as in Project A except gold is used for accent color, and paper towels are used for texture

METHOD

1. Cut a strip 2¼-inches wide from your plastic material. Measure and cut to fit, then staple three or four times across ends to join. Cover staples with masking tape inside and outside.

2. Cover both edges of band with masking tape, fringing to turn over edges smoothly.

3. Tear textured paper towels into approximately 1-inch squares. Completely cover inside and outside of band, using diluted white glue. Overlap the squares a fraction for an interesting effect. Paint with diluted glue and allow to dry thoroughly.

4. Twist two long strands of cord together and glue around the edges of bracelet. Use full-strength glue, pressing cord in place with your fingers. Twist two more strands together and glue cord in "drum" pattern as in illustration.

5. When cord is dry, paint entire bracelet with white titanium. Let dry.

6. Give one coat of pink or rose. Dry.

7. Make a gold wash, using gold Bronzing powder and turpentine. Brush lightly over all surfaces of bracelet including the cord. Let dry.

8. Highlight cord and some surfaces of bracelet with gold jeweler's paste.

9. One coat of gloss varnish. Dry.

10. Finish with a coat of clear lacquer spray. Dry.

11. Glue one large pink glass jewel at one end of each panel, alternating around the bracelet (see illustration). Use Bond cement.

## E - *GREEN AND GOLD BRACELET

This is an unusually easy bracelet to make. It is simple in design yet very attractive and looks expensive.

MATERIALS

The materials are the same as Project A with these exceptions:
Green acrylic paint, gold paint, yellow glass blobs

METHOD

Follow steps in Project A, except paint bracelet inside and outside with green acrylic. Use a gold wash to antique it inside and outside, and highlight the cord with gold jeweler's paste. Give three coats of gloss varnish, drying well between coats. Glue yellow glass blobs with Bond cement inside curves of cord.

## F - IVORY AND GOLD BRACELET

A little more ornate than the others in design, this bracelet is fit for a princess.

MATERIALS

Approximately the same as for Project A, except for different colors

METHOD

1. Make the bracelet base in the same way as Project A. Use finer cord so it will be easier to make the scroll-like loops and decorations. Make several of the loops large enough to accommodate the large size faceted glass jewels.
2. When cord is dry, paint with ivory. (Add a tiny amount of yellow to white titanium.) Dry well.
3. Make a thin antique wash using black. Brush wash over all surfaces of bracelet, wiping off most of it so that just the joinings of the paper squares will show a little of the black. Dry well.
4. Paint cord with gold paint. Dry.
5. Give two coats of gloss varnish, drying well between coats.
6. For a very hard, glossy finish, coat with Joli Glaze.
7. When dry, use Bond cement to glue blue and white faceted glass jewels inside loops and beside curves of cord. Use square, round and oval shaped jewels.

## G - PINK PRINCESS BRACELET

MATERIALS

The same as in Project A

METHOD

Make this bracelet the same as Project F, the Ivory and Gold Bracelet, but paint it with shocking pink. Give it a black antique wash and when dry, highlight with gold jeweler's paste rubbed over the cording. Glue pale pink stones of various shape into loops and curves of cord with Bond cement.

## H - GOLD AND TOPAZ SLAVE BRACELET

### MATERIALS

Materials are the same as in Project A with the addition of Gook, burnt umber, and large topaz or yellow glass blobs. Also paper towels

### METHOD

1. Cut a bleach bottle strip about 1½-inches wide, measure length, cut, staple and cover staples and edges with masking tape.

2. Tear large squares of paper towel. Glue onto inside and outside surfaces of band with diluted glue. Paint with remainder of glue and allow to dry.

3. Squeeze Gook directly from the tube onto the edges of bracelet and in the center to resemble cord. Make circles large enough to accommodate the large glass blobs you plan to use.

*Fig. 31   Beautiful bracelets, continued. Left to right. back row, H, I; front row, K, L. Designed by Lura Smith.*

4. When dry, paint with white titanium over all. Dry.

5. Give one coat of burnt umber or brown. Dry.

6. Accent the raised pattern with gold jeweler's paste, covering it heavily. Also rub the gold paste over the remaining surfaces of the bracelet.

7. Give two or three coats of gloss varnish, drying well between coats.

8. For a good, hard seal, spray with clear lacquer or coat with Joli Glaze.

9. When well dried, glue topaz or yellow crackle-glass blobs into circles outlined. Use Bond cement.

## I - EMERALD AND SILVER BRACELET

This bracelet is made in the same way as Project C except silver tea paper is used, the cord is highlighted with silver jeweler's paste and green and white square and oval glass jewels are used.

## J - SILVER AND BLACK BRACELET

White pearls with aurora borealis leaves add up to a stunning and different bracelet.

### MATERIALS

Same as for Project A

### METHOD

1. Cut plastic band, staple and cover edges with masking tape.

2. Using diluted glue, cover outside of band with newspaper squares cut about ½-inch square. Place masking tape the exact width of band on inside surface. Coat with glue and dry well.

3. Give two coats of white titanium, drying well between coats.

4. Paint with silver paint inside and out.

5. When dry, glue covered silver wire braid with full-strength glue to edges of bracelet. Glue it in a running design down the center, twisting it into loops large enough to hold the pearls you will use.

6. When dry, paint center design with black, using a fine camel's hair brush. Dry thoroughly. See color plate VIII.

7. Apply a thin black wash to antique the inside and outside sur-

faces of the bracelet. Give three coats of gloss varnish. Dry well.

8. When thoroughly dry, glue on jewels with Bond cement. White pearls go inside the loops with aurora borealis oval faceted jewels for the leaves.

## K - SILVER BRACELET

This bracelet looks different and is very lovely with purple and pink jewels.

MATERIALS

Same as for Project A

METHOD

1. Use the same steps as for Project A, except glue *several coats* of newspaper squares to the outer surface of the bracelet, letting each coat dry before adding another. In this way, build up a thick layer, heavier in the center and with rounded edges.

2. When bracelet has dried well, coat with white titanium. Dry.

3. Glue pre-shrunk cord in wide scallops down center of band, using full-strength glue.

4. When dry, paint with medium silver wash. Let dry.

5. Highlight cord with silver jeweler's paste or paint with silver paint.

6. When dry, glue on small purple rhinestones and oval pink glass jewels as in illustration, using Bond cement.

## L - RED AND WHITE BRACELET

This is an outstanding design, sure to bring compliments from all who see it. Beautiful with a red, white or navy suit.

MATERIALS

Same as for Project A

METHOD

1. Cut plastic bleach bottle strip, staple and edge with masking tape.

2. Glue newspaper squares to outside of bracelet, using diluted white glue.

3. Line inside surface of bracelet with narrow strips of newspaper, overlapping them. Or use masking tape if you wish. Coat with glue and dry.

4. When dry, give two coats of white titanium, drying well between coats.

5. Using full-strength glue place heavy cord around edges and in a curving design down center of bracelet (see illustration).

6. When cord is dry, paint inside surface of bracelet bright red. Paint cord silver.

7. Make silver wash using silver powder and turpentine. Apply to outside of bracelet for antique effect. Let dry.

8. Give one coat gloss varnish. Let dry.

9. Glue square red and white faceted glass jewels into curves of the cord with Bond cement. See illustration.

## INSTANT PAPIER-MACHE BRACELETS AND OTHERS

These beautiful bracelets are light and very expensive looking, yet so simple to make you will be amazed. Earrings to match are the next project, and you may want to make a pair at the same time you make a bracelet.

MATERIALS

 Plastic bleach bottle, scissors
 Instant Papier-mache mix or homemade papier-mache (see Basic
  Formula II and III)
 Stapler, masking tape, newspaper or paper towels
 White wood glue, water, bowl, spoon, plastic bags, wax paper
 Acrylic paints: various colors, gloss varnish
 Gold and silver Venus Bronzing powders and medium
 Turpentine, cord or Gook, burlap braid
 Gold and silver jeweler's paste

## M - VIOLET AND GOLD SLAVE BRACELET

 Materials as needed from list above

METHOD

1. Cut strip from bleach bottle 2¼-inches wide. Measure around fist cutting length needed, staple, and cover edges with masking tape.

2. Tear or cut large squares of paper towel, use diluted white glue and cover inside surface of bracelet, overlapping rows and bringing them neatly to edges of band. (See Project A, this chapter.)

3. Mix Instant papier-mache mix according to directions on package or make Formula II. Mixing in a plastic bag will save mess. Do not make too much. About one cup should be enough.

4. Apply a layer of the mix, building up the center portion a quarter-inch or more, patting it smooth. Leave enough texture for interest when it is antiqued. Cover entire outside of bracelet.

5. While still very wet, impress a circle design with a bottle cap or other round object. Leave a raised ridge around the circle for interest. Be sure center of circle is flat so you can glue jewels to it. This is difficult to do if the surface is rounded. Make five or six circles at even distances apart around bracelet. Place on wax paper to dry overnight or until it is completely hard and dry.

6. When dry, give a coat of white titanium inside and out. Let dry.

7. Paint inside and out with violet or purple paint. Let dry. Examine to see if any white spots show through. If so, give a second coat of color.

8. When completely dry, make a thin gold antique wash using gold powder and turpentine. Apply to inside and outside surfaces of bracelet. Dry thoroughly on wax paper. Highlight with gold jeweler's paste.

9. Coat with gloss varnish. Dry well.

10. Glue alternate round and square amethyst faceted glass jewels, or use all round or all square jewels, to center of circles. Use Bond cement.


N - GREEN AND ORANGE WITH GOLD

Although no jewels are used for this bracelet, the psychedelic colors are striking. Make it in pink and purple, yellow and red, or any combination of colors you like.

METHOD

1. Measure and cut one-inch strip from bleach bottle, staple and cover edges with masking tape, as in Project A.

2. Cover inside of bracelet with masking tape to make smooth surface.

3. Mix instant papier-mache mix according to directions or make Basic Formula II. About one cup should be enough.

4. Pile thick pieces of the mix to band surface, smoothing and shaping as you apply, making the surface quite high and rounded. Smooth edges neatly.

5. When bracelet surface is to your liking, use a knife or other straight edge to impress a zig-zag line evenly around the center of bracelet. Be sure the marks are wide enough for the cord you will glue in later. Dry on wax paper overnight or until completely hard.

6. Use full-strength white glue to saturate cord. Press cord firmly into zig-zag design. Let dry.

7. When completely dry, give a coat of white titanium inside and out. Push paint down into cord and any crevice of design. Let dry.

8. Paint one side of the zig-zag pattern with orange, working the paint into one side of the cord only, so no white will show through. Let dry, then paint the other side with green, also working it into the other side of the cord, leaving cord white on top. Paint inside of bracelet either orange or green. Dry thoroughly.

9. Make a rich gold wash using gold powder and turpentine. Coat the entire bracelet, getting as much gold on cord as possible.

10. When dry, highlight with gold jeweler's paste.

11. Give one or more coats of gloss varnish. Let dry thoroughly before wearing.

Earrings to match are given in Project C, this chapter.

## O - EXOTIC GOLD AND TOPAZ BRACELET

This bracelet is excitingly different, exotic and brilliant. It is lovely done in white rhinestone "diamonds" instead of the topaz or amber, and would be outstanding using jewels of any color.

MATERIALS

The materials as needed from under Instant Papier Mache Bracelets

METHOD

1. Obtain a strip of decorative burlap braid from a hobby shop or yardage store. Cut bleach bottle strip the exact width of braid. Cut plastic strip to proper length (measured over your doubled fist), staple across cut edges three times and cover edges with masking tape (as in Project A).

2. Cover inside and outside of band with newspaper squares glued on with diluted white glue. Let dry.

3. Soak burlap braid, cut a little longer than needed for band, in diluted glue and allow to dry on wax paper.

4. Using full-strength white glue, glue braid to bracelet, joining the ends as neatly as possible. Let dry thoroughly.

5. Paint inside surface of bracelet with white titanium. Dry.

6. Make a medium mixture of gold paint, using gold powder and liquid medium. Paint braid with gold, giving two coats to cover well. Paint inside surface of bracelet with gold also. Dry thoroughly.

7. Give three coats of gloss varnish inside and out, drying well between coats.

8. When bracelet is thoroughly dry, glue large topaz or amber colored rhinestones in the natural circles of the braid, using Bond cement. Glue four small matching rhinestones at the four corners of the circle. This makes a brilliant and most unusual bracelet.

*Fig. 32   Bracelets of instant and homemade papier-mache. Left to right: back row, M, N, O; front row, P, Q. M, N and Q designed by author.*

## P - TURQUOISE AND GOLD BRACELET

1. Cut a strip from a bleach bottle about one-inch wide and the proper length for your wrist. Or use a cardboard tube base of the right size. If you use the plastic, staple joining edges three times across cut, then cover staples and band edges with masking tape.

2. Cover inside of band with masking tape or glue on newspaper squares with diluted glue. Let dry.

3. Prepare instant papier-mache mix into a very thin mixture or make Formula II. About one cup should be enough. Pat the mix on the bracelet surface and make a very smooth surface. Cover bracelet edges with the mix, too, rounding edges smoothly. Check illustration for this. Let dry on wax paper.

4. Glue cord with full-strength white glue in a graceful looped design as shown. Let dry.

5. Apply one coat of white titanium. Dry well.

6. Apply one coat of turquoise. Let dry. Highlight cord with gold jeweler's paste.

7. Give one coat of gloss varnish. Dry.

8. Apply one coat of clear lacquer spray or Joli Glaze. Dry thoroughly.

9. Using Bond cement, glue aurora borealis faceted glass jewels in loops of cord.

## Q - AMETHYST AND SILVER BRACELET

This bracelet, made from a masking tape tube, is so simple to make that it is a good one to start a youngster on.

MATERIALS

Materials as needed from list on page 71

METHOD

1. Use a masking tape tube or similar tube the correct size for your wrist.

2. Glue newspaper squares over the outside surface (see Project A). Dry.

3. Use full-strength white glue to glue cord around edges. Dry well.

4. Paint band inside and out with white titanium. Dry.

5. Paint with one coat of light pink or orchid. Dry.

6. Make a thin silver wash using silver powder and turpentine. Paint inner and outer surfaces of bracelet. This is the antique coat and will go on unevenly. Dry well.

7. Highlight cord at edges of bracelet with silver jeweler's paste. Dry.

8. Coat with one or two layers of gloss varnish, drying well between coats.

9. Using Bond cement, glue large amethyst glass jewels around band, interspersing small white beads or pearls between them. (See illustration.)

## FOUR PAIR OF EARRINGS

Earrings to match your papier-mache bracelets will give you unusually high-style sets. They are lightweight and easy to wear. Fair warning! If you make one pair you'll make a dozen!

### MATERIALS

The materials needed for earrings are exactly the same as for the bracelets with the exception of earring backs. Old ones can be used, so save old costume jewelry and collect odd earrings from friends. Earring back findings can be purchased at hobby shops or the dime store.

## A - AMETHYST AND GOLD

1. Cut a circle from bleach bottle plastic. Hold them to your ear and look in the mirror to make sure they are the right size.

2. Prepare instant papier-mache mix or make a small amount of Formula II. You will probably make these at the same time you make a bracelet so you will use some of the left-over mix.

3. Make a small ball of the material and flatten it onto the plastic circle. Shape it to have sloping sides, mounded in the center. Make three small depressions around the center in which to place jewels later. Let dry.

4. When thoroughly dry, see if mix is set firmly on the plastic. If not, remove and glue firmly with Bond cement or full-strength white glue.

5. Paint front and back of earring buttons with white titanium. Dry on wax paper.

6. Paint with purple or violet. Dry.

7. Highlight with gold jeweler's paste. Give one coat of gloss varnish. Let dry.

8. Glue earring backs to plastic side of buttons using Bond cement and placing the backs a little above center. The earring findings should always be the same color as you use for highlighting: gold color backs with gold highlights, silver backs with silver highlights.

9. Use Bond cement to glue two pearls and an amethyst or purple jewel to each earring. These earrings have an amethyst crescent jewel with two white pearls and match the purple and gold slave bracelet, Project M. However, by varying the colors of paint and jewels used, you can match any bracelet you prefer.

## B    RED AND GOLD EARRINGS

These beautiful earrings match the red and gold bracelet given earlier, and both are shown in color.

1. Cut two round disks about the size of a quarter from fairly heavy cardboard such as tablet backing.

2. Build up top surface of both circles with instant papier-mache mix to make a shallow domed effect. Let dry thoroughly.

3. Cover back and front of buttons with ¼-inch newspaper squares, using diluted white glue. Turn squares down over edges to back. Dry.

4. Paint front and back with white titanium. Dry.

5. Give one coat of gold paint.

6. When dry, use Bond cement to glue flat side of button to gold colored earring backs, placing a little above center of button.

7. Give one coat of Joli Glaze. Dry well.

8. Glue two square red glass jewels and two oval shaped gold jewels to earring front using Bond cement.

## C - GOLD AND ORANGE EARRINGS

The backings for this pair of earrings were taken from a used pair which had lost some of the stones. The backings had a flat surface with a raised edge which made the papier-mache very easy to shape. They match the two bracelets described earlier.

METHOD

1. Shape a round ball of papier-mache mix, either instant mix or Formula II. Make the ball a little smaller than the earring back. (If you do not have an old pair of earring backings you can use, cut a disk from bleach bottle plastic the size you wish and form the papier-mache mix on it.) Press ball down firmly to fit exactly the metal backing or plastic disk. Shape and pinch the sides and top of ball to roughly form a flower shape, punching a flat depression in the center large enough to hold the size jewel you wish to use. Pinch pointed flower petal shapes (see illustration). Make both earrings as nearly as possible the same size and shape. Allow to dry thoroughly on wax paper.

2. When dry, test to see if the material is firmly adhering to the backing. If not, remove and glue on with Bond cement.

3. Paint with white titanium. If metal backing is used, do not paint it, but if plastic disk, paint it the same as the papier-mache buttons.

4. When dry, paint with orange. Dry.

5. Highlight with gold jeweler's paste.

6. Give one coat of gloss varnish. Dry well.

7. Place a drop of Bond cement in depression of buttons and place a large orange or pink faceted glass jewel in each. Or use any other color you like.

## D - DROP EARRINGS

An interesting pair of earrings which you can make to match any outfit you own. Match a bracelet or necklace, too, while you're at it!

MATERIALS

Instant Mix or Formula II
18-gauge wire, jeweler's pliers
Earring backs with drop loop
Acrylic paints, wax paper

METHOD

1. Cut two identical lengths of 18-gauge wire 5½- to 6-inches long or the size and length you wish.

2. Make a small loop at one end of the wire with a pair of jeweler's pliers, then shape the wire into an elongated diamond like the ones illustrated. However, you can make yours round, a straight triangle, or any other shape.

3. Twist end of wire into the loop to finish and hold the shape desired. You may wish to hang a bead or a second smaller loop inside the larger drops. If so, fasten it into the loop now.

4. Roll small amounts of papier-mache mix to form elongated rolls or "snakes" to fit on wires. Indent these rolls with your finger-nail or a knife down the center and press them over the wire, smoothing the edges as you go. When both earring wires are covered, lay them on wax paper to dry.

5. When thoroughly dried, turn earrings over and press more of the mixture on the back so wire will be neatly covered on both sides. Press two small balls of mix into cups of earring backs. Dry well.

6. Paint with any color paint. Dry.

7. Attach drop shapes to loop of earring backs.

*Fig. 33 Four pair of earrings to match your bracelets. Left to right: button earrings A, B, C; drop earrings D.*

# 7.

## OTHER BANGLES, BAUBLES
## AND BEADS

A girl can never have too many "bangles, baubles and beads". These are so attractive and so much fun to make that you will never tire of them. For gifts they are unsurpassed, and as small craft projects any group will be immediately enthusiastic. Try one and see for yourself!

### BLACK-EYED SUZAN PIN

A huge pin, 5½-inches across, the black-eyed Suzan in figure 34 makes a stunning accessory.

#### MATERIALS

> Shirt cardboard or similar light weight cardboard
> Beige and black matte Swistraw (see Glossary)
> Crochet hook #8 or H
> Acrylic paints: white titanium, beige, black
> ½-inch camel's hair artist's brush, white glue
> Pin backing
> Large shallow bowl

METHOD

1. Cut two eight-petalled flowers from thin cardboard. If you will look at the illustration you will see that the petals are oval and pointed. Draw two circles with a compass or by tying a piece of string to a pencil. Make the first circle small—the size you will want the center or eye of the flower to be. Then make the larger circle around it in the radius of 5½-inches. Draw or cut the pointed petals from the edge of the outside circle to the center. Make two of these sets of petals, the same size.

2. Prepare diluted white glue in a large, shallow bowl. Soak one set of the petals until it is damp but not saturated with the glue. Lift from glue to a sheet of wax paper and shape the petals by pushing from the end of the petal toward the center, making them curve slightly. Allow to dry on the wax paper, shaping occasionally until the shape holds. Repeat with the second set of petals.

3. When dry, glue pin back with full-strength white glue slightly above the center back of one set of petals. Cover the base or shank of the metal pin with several newspaper squares. Dry.

4. Paint both sides of both sets of petals with white titanium. Let dry.

5. Mix beige paint beginning with white and adding yellow, brown and black to get the shade to match your beige Swistraw.

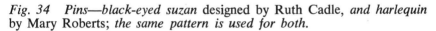

*Fig. 34   Pins—black-eyed suzan* designed by Ruth Cadle, *and harlequin* by Mary Roberts; *the same pattern is used for both.*

Instead of beige, you can make your flower pin yellow, white, or any other color, but be sure to use matching Swistraw.

6. Paint both sides of both sets of petals with beige. Let dry thoroughly.

7. Antique both by dry-brushing with black. To do this, dip brush into black paint, wipe most of it off with a soft cloth, then brush each petal lightly from center of flower to petal tip, making the stroke lighter as you get to the tip. Dry well before next step.

8. Give both two coats of matte varnish, drying well between coats.

9. Use #8 or H crochet hook to crochet beige Swistraw into a chain about two yards long, measuring before breaking it off to see if it will reach completely around each petal of the flower, outlining it in an unbroken chain (see illustration). Make two chains the same length.

10. Glue each chain with full-strength white glue to the outside edges of petals, completely outlining them. Let dry thoroughly.

11. Make a crocheted chain about two yards long with black Swistraw.

12. Place a large blob of full-strength white glue into the center of flower having the pin backing glued to it. Place the second flower on the blob of glue, taking care to alternate the petals so all can be seen. Press down firmly and let dry.

13. Use full-strength white glue to make a firm, coiled "eye" in the center of the pin with the black chain.

## HARLEQUIN PIN

A riot of crazy-quilt tissue paper scraps was used for the decorative dress accessory in figure 34. It is an eye-catching 5½ inches in diameter.

MATERIALS

Same pattern as Black-eyed Suzan pin, above
Shirt cardboard or similar type
Small multicolored scraps of tissue paper ¼-inch to 1 or 2 inches in size
Green gloss Swistraw, white glue, white titanium paint
Pin back, glue, small brush, shallow bowl

METHOD

1. Cut two petal patterns from cardboard as in project given just before this one.

2. Soak paper flowers in diluted glue to dampen, but not saturate. Remove and curl or twist petals backward (see illustration). Let dry on wax paper, picking up to curl petals from time to time until they hold.

3. Glue pin back slightly above center back of one flower with full-strength glue. Let dry.

4. Paint both sides of both flowers with white titanium. Dry.

5. Cut small scraps of all colors of tissue (you never throw anything away in papier-mache). Have varying sizes and colors arranged for easy picking up with your glue brush.

6. Brush petals of flower with diluted glue and lay tissue scraps on it, overlapping the colors to give even a third color if you like, which will also add texture and interest. Cover both sides of both flowers. Cover pin shank with tissue also so that it becomes part of the flower. Dry well.

7. Brush with two coats of gloss varnish, covering both sides of both flowers. Dry well between coats.

8. Glue the two flowers together with full-strength glue, alternating petals of front and back flower for best effect. Dry.

9. Make a pompon of the green Swistraw about 1¾-inches in diameter by bunching short lengths of the Swistraw (about 2-inches long) into a compact bundle then tying very tightly in the center. Double the cut ends together and trim to a rounded shape. Glue this pompon into the center of your harlequin pin with full-strength glue.

## BUTTERFLY PIN

So vivid alight on your suit or dress! Give it the natural coloration of a particular species, or color it wild to suit your own designing mood.

MATERIALS

Shirt cardboard, two wooden stick matches
Plastic fibres for feelers

Pin backing, fine cord, white glue
Acrylic paints: burnt umber, yellow, red, black, white titanium, or
your own colors

METHOD

1. Cut matches into two 1½-inch lengths. Glue together with full-strength glue to make body.
2. Wrap sticks with cord, gluing with full-strength glue as you wrap. Twist and secure end of strand with glue. Place on wax paper to dry.
3. Before glue is completely dry on the "body", force two plastic "feelers" into the head end of body, dipping fibres into glue first. (If you cannot get the plastic fibres at a hobby shop, perhaps you could use some from a plastic broom.) Dry well.
4. When body is completely dry, paint with black, touching just the end of the feelers with the black. Let dry.
5. Fold cardboard and cut two pair of wings. See illustration for shape. It would be very helpful if you could find the colored picture of a butterfly to follow for your pattern. For the pin shown in figure 35, the large pair of wings are 3⅛-inches wide and 2½-inches high at the outer tips, tapering to ¾-inch at center body. The smaller wing is about 2-inches long at the outer edge, tapering to ½-inch at center body and is 2⅛-inches wide. The size is suggested here, but you may wish to make the pin larger or smaller.
6. Paint the two sets of wings before assembling. First give two coats of white titanium, drying between coats. Then paint both sides of wings with burnt umber for background color. Dry.
7. Outline outer edges of large upper wings with black, then paint in the design. Paint only the lower point of small wings black. See illustration for design.
8. Paint red dots to accent wings, also use a few small stripes of yellow at the top of wings.
9. When completely dry, glue wings together, placing the large pair on top of the smaller, lower ones, so that the center portion is about 1-inch wide.
10. Glue body on top of wings with the head protruding about ¼-inch above the "V" of top wings. Dry.
11. Brush with two coats of matte varnish, drying between coats.
12. When fully dry, glue pin back finding to back of butterfly a little above center. When dry, the butterfly pin is ready to wear.

## *LADYBUG PIN

"Ladybug, Ladybug, fly away home!" Everyone knows the old children's rhyme. But for this Ladybug (figure 35), "home" is a lady's suit or dress. Easy to make, the pin measures 2¼ by 1¾ inches.

### MATERIALS

Shirt cardboard, white glue
Instant papier-mache mix or Formula II
Pin back one-inch size
Acrylic paints: white titanium, black, red, gloss varnish
Wax paper, plastic bag

### METHOD

1. Cut an elongated oval from cardboard measuring approximately 2½-inches long by 1¾ inches wide, tapering in slightly at the "head" end.
2. Glue the metal pin back across the body about one-inch below the head end, using full-strength white glue. Let dry before doing any further work.
3. Mix a small amount of instant mix or Formula II in a plastic bag. Place mixture in a small mound on top of the cardboard shape

*Fig. 35    Ladybug and butterfly pins.*

(the pin is on the back), and shape the body as illustrated. Curve up the head end making two bulges for "eyes". Dry well. Save some of the mix in the plastic bag in the refrigerator for use later.

4. When top is dry, cover the underside of pin, including the metal shank, with a thin layer of the papier-mache mixture. Be careful not to get any of it into the hinge or safety catch.

5. When pin is completely dry, paint both top and underside with white titanium acrylic. Dry.

6. Paint top side of "Ladybug" with red, making two curved wings as illustrated. Dry.

7. Paint underside with black. Dry.

8. Turn pin over and paint head and lower section which shows through wings at bottom with black. Paint black dots on wings. Let dry.

9. Give two coats of gloss varnish on both sides, drying well between coats.

### *FABULOUS BEADS

These resemble antique rose beads. Perhaps you may want to put cologne in the papier-mache mixture to make the resemblance even greater. Or make them larger, paint them bright blue, and you will have Donkey Beads without the heavy weight. (See figure 36.)

MATERIALS

> Instant papier-mache mix or Formula II
> Bowl, spoon, shoe box, white glue
> 18-gauge floral wire
> Wax paper, plastic bag
> Acrylic paints: white titanium and any color
> Cord, acrylic gloss varnish
> Gold jeweler's paste (optional)

METHOD

1. Mix a small amount of instant mix, following directions on the package. About one cup of the dry preparation before adding water should be enough. Make in plastic bag to avoid muss. 54 beads in graduated sizes were made to create the 14-inch string shown in the illustration.

2. Decide on the size beads you want to make. Beads will shrink

*VIII. Jeweled treasure chest, page 42; bracelets and other jewelry, pages 58-101.*

IX. Above: *Treasured bowls made from trash (all described in Chapter 8, page 102)—footed bowl from an old brass oriental bowl; fruit bowl from a woven basket; gold-leaf nut bowl or candy dish.* X. Below: *"Little girl" figurine spray-can cover, page 28; gold hand mirror, page 32; jeweled standing mirror, page 35.*

as they dry, so make them a little larger to allow for this.

3. Roll a bit of mix in palm of your hand to make bead round and the size you want. When you have made the number you need, working on wax paper, push the 18-gauge floral wire (may be obtained at dime store) through the exact center of beads. String them on the wire until it is filled, but do not allow the wet beads to touch. Rotate beads to make small even hole for stringing and hang wire across the shoe box to dry. As beads dry, turn them on the wire to prevent the beads sagging or sticking to the wire.

4. When beads are thoroughly dry (this may take a day or two), brush them with one coat of diluted white glue while still on the wire. This will seal the papier-mache and keep it from absorbing the paint.

5. When dry, paint beads (still on the wire) with color desired. The ones pictured are olive green. Dry well.

6. Highlight with gold jeweler's paste. The beads illustrated were not smoothed after drying since the rough texture was desired. However, if you want them smoother, rub with sandpaper before painting.

7. Before removing from wire, coat beads with several applications of gloss varnish, drying well between coats.

8. When completely dry remove from wires. Thread a darning needle that will fit through the hole in the beads with medium weight cord the length you will need. String beads. If you have graduated your bead sizes, arrange them on wax paper in the order you wish, then string the smaller ones first with larger ones graduating to the center, then gradually the smaller ones again. Tie the ends of the string together when all beads are strung, making a good strong knot. Pull knot inside the bead closest so it won't show.

Youngsters will adore making these strings of beads. Paint them all colors of the rainbow, buy long shoestrings and keep them in a box for your favorite young ones to string them on. Caution note: the beads are not meant to be eaten!

Earrings to match are the next project.

## DROP EARRINGS TO MATCH BEADS

MATERIALS

Materials are the same as for preceding project with these additions:
Earring finding: drop earring backs having metal loop

*Fig. 36   Jewelry, described on pages 96-101. Left to right: bib necklace, fabulous beads, matching earrings (above left), psychedelic medallion.*

METHOD

1. Use six small beads made in the same manner or at the same time as beads in project listed above. In addition make two small beads without holes and push them firmly into the cup of the earring finding. Dry well.

2. Finish in the same way as beads.

3. Use the same heavy thread or cord and darning needle as for necklace. First thread a small pearl or colored glass bead (same color as earrings), then double cord and string on three of the papier-mache beads. Tie cord through loop on earring back and pull the knot through the top bead so it will not show. (See figure 36.)

## MEDALLION

Making this bauble is like making mud pies, but what a difference—who hangs a mud pie around his neck! You can work it in various motifs—a psychedelic dream symbol, an Indian spirit charm, family crest, religious motif, or whatever.

MATERIALS

Instant mix or Formula II, bowl, spoon or plastic bag
White glue, wax paper, acrylic paints
Gold, silver or brass chain, jump rings
Pliers

METHOD

1. Mix papier-mache according to directions on the package if you use the instant mix, or consult Basic Formula II directions for the homemade type. A plastic bag is handy to mix small amounts. One-half cup of the mixture should be sufficient.

2. Pat out the shape you wish on a piece of waxed paper. It can be round, square or any other shape. See illustration. Flip the wet form over and press smooth on the other side, working with it until you get the shape you want. (Just like mud pies!)

3. Cut a 4-inch length of chain with pliers. Place the chain across the top of the medallion and press it into the moist material being careful not to destroy the shape you have made. Leave enough chain hanging out of each side to use later for attaching to your cord. Imbed the chain and cover it with the papier-mache.

4. Place medallion out of the way to dry for two or three days. Length of time it takes to dry will depend on the thickness of the piece and temperature and humidity of weather. Do not place it in the sun or near heat as this may cause it to warp or twist out of shape. Slow drying is best. It will dry on wax paper without sticking.

5. When thoroughly dry give both sides two coats of white titanium, drying between coats.

6. Sketch design on medallion with pencil or use carbon paper to transfer a design. Paint, being careful to allow colors to dry before adding a color near to it so colors will not run together.

7. When well dried coat with matte varnish, brushing on several coats, drying between coats.

8. Attach ends of embedded chain to a jump ring (jewelry finding) and attach this to the longer length of chain to go around neck. A leather thong, rope or ribbon can be used for this. A Swistraw cord was used for the medallion pictured.

## BIB NECKLACE

Here again you can have the massive look without weight which makes papier-mache jewelry so desirable and easy to wear.

MATERIALS

Cardboard, wax paper, white glue

Instant mix or Formula I, plastic bag
Ten ¼-inch jump rings (jewelry findings)
Six jump rings slightly smaller than ¼-inch
Modeling paste, silver jeweler's paste
Acrylic paints; black, matte varnish
Chain with clasp

METHOD

1. Cut five patterns from cardboard: two small, two medium and one large for center. (See figure 36 for shape.)

2. Mix about two cups of papier-mache and roll or pat mixture between two sheets of wax paper until it is smooth.

3. Lift off the top sheet of wax paper and lay cardboard patterns on the dough-like mixture. Use a silver knife to cut around pattern, scraping away the excess papier-mache. Push ¼-inch jump rings into the top corners on back of each piece. Leave half of rings visible at sides, cover rest with papier-mache mixture. Or wait until Step 5 to do this.

4. When cutting is finished, remove cardboard patterns and smooth edges of medallions. Allow to dry thoroughly away from sun or warm place. This may take a day or two, depending on thickness of your sections and the weather. The pieces will curve slightly while drying, but this is all right. Keep checking them from time to time to be sure they keep the proper shape. The slight curve gives a softer look to the finished necklace.

5. When pieces are completely dry, place rounded side down and glue the larger jump ring to each side, if you have not already done this, at the top, using full-strength white glue. Dry well before handling. The jump rings are now on the back of the medallion sections.

6. Coat each piece, front and back, with one coat of diluted white glue and allow to dry on wax paper.

7. Use a clean brush and paint the design you wish on each medallion front with modeling paste. A scroll effect was used for the ones illustrated, one that lends itself well to highlighting. Be sure modeling paste is not too thick. If it tends to leave brush marks, dilute with water. You may want to texture the medallions with your fingers or in other ways. Dry well.

8. When dry, turn pieces over and brush back with modeling paste. Dry.

9. Paint both sides with black, drying before turning to paint other side.

10. When medallions are thoroughly dry, highlight them with silver jeweler's paste to bring out the texture and design. When dry, buff well with a soft cloth.

11. Apply matte varnish to both sides of each piece, give several coats, drying well between coats.

12. When dry, place necklace medallions in order desired and link together with the slightly smaller jump rings. With another jump ring at each of the side sections, attach to chain ends having clasp in center back.

# 8.

## TRAYS, BOWLS AND BASKETS

Decorator pieces from cast-offs! Here are articles you can never have too many of—for kitchen, dining room, patio, and even, when they are as beautiful and unusual as these, as accent pieces in the living room.

### ANTIQUED GREEN AND GOLD SERVING TRAY

Do you have an old wooden tray much the worse for wear? Or a large ceramic plate that is cracked or chipped? This is an excellent way to salvage it (figure 38).

MATERIALS

> Wooden tray or large ceramic plate
> Newspaper squares, white glue
> Pre-shrunk cord, gold jeweler's paste
> Acrylic paints: chartreuse green, chromium oxide green, black, purple
> Clear lacquer spray or Joli glaze

METHOD

1. Cut newspaper into 2-inch squares. If you are using a cracked plate, force full-strength glue into the crack and build up any chips

*Fig. 37   Green and gold serving tray,* before—

with a small wad of newspaper soaked in glue. Be sure surface is smooth.

2. Using diluted glue, begin gluing squares at the outside edge. Work in a circular pattern toward the center. Overlap the first row of squares, slash those at the edge so they will fit smoothly, turned over the edge to the back. Cover front of tray completely and allow to dry.

3. When front is dry, turn tray over and cover back in the same way, excepting the edges which will already be covered. End with one square in the center back. Let dry.

4. Decide on pattern; glue pre-shrunk cord over penciled-on design. The tray shown has a large flower design in the center. This can be duplicated by first placing a 1½-inch circle in the exact center of tray, then radiating 7 petals from the circle outline. Cut 7 lengths of pre-shrunk cord and glue over petal outlines and circle, using full-strength glue. Make scalloped, looped border in the same way, about ¾-inch from edge. Press glued cord firmly and let dry.

5. Paint entire tray front and back with white titanium acrylic. Let dry.

6. Paint front and back with chartreuse green acrylic. The chartreuse will be the background color for the back of tray, front border and inside the loops of cord scallop. Work paint into base of cord scallops at edge and inside loops. Let dry.

7. Paint center circle purple, flower petals, and remaining portion of tray inside scalloped borders a blue-green. Work all of these colors carefully into the base of cord bordering them so that no white will show later when cord is dry.

8. When thoroughly dry, make a thin wash with black and brush over entire tray, front and back, wiping off with soft cloth to give the antique effect. Dry.

9. Cover cord with gold jeweler's paste, rubbing on with finger, or paint cord with gold paint. Highlight inside petals and circle of flower design with a little of the gold paste if you wish.

*Fig. 38    Serving tray in Fig. 37—the* after *view*. By Lura Smith.

10. Apply two coats of gloss varnish, drying well between coats, to finish.

11. If tray is to be used extensively, a coat of Joli glaze will give a more durable finish.

12. If tray is to be used for serving foods and liquids, spray on a heavy coating of furniture wax. This will also tone down the shiny finish somewhat.

## OBLONG GOLD TRAY

A decorative treasure (figure 39) can be made from an old tin serving tray ready for the dump. Good places to find discarded trays and bowls are rummage sales, patio and garage sales, and flea markets. Happy hunting!

MATERIALS

> Metal tray, white glue
> Gold Japanese tea paper, Joli glaze
> Acrylic paints: burnt umber, Mars black
> 2-inch brush

*Fig. 39 The oblong gold tray and the tray ready to be salvaged; and the gold-leaf bonbon bowl.*

METHOD

1. If there are any rust spots on the tray, remove with steel wool.

2. Make two very thin washes by adding water to the burnt umber and Mars black in separate bowls.

3. Spread a full sheet of the gold tea paper on newspapers and spatter with first the black wash, then the brown. Do this by dipping the brush in and "flipping" or dropping the paint on in large puddles. Experiment first with a small piece of the paper to decide how to get the effect you want. Rinse brush in clear water and blend washes together to mingle the colors. When the gold paper is antiqued to your satisfaction, allow to dry.

4. When paper is dry, tear into irregular squares 1 to 3 inches in size, varying sizes and shapes of squares. (See illustration.)

5. Use diluted glue to apply squares to tray. The gold will run while gluing, so try not to get it too wet. However, if the silver base color shows through the gold here and there, it only adds to the beauty of the tray. Turn edges of tray very neatly and cover back of tray also. Let dry thoroughly.

6. When tray is thoroughly dry, coat with three layers of Joli glaze, drying well between coats.

## SALVAGING AN OLD TRAY

If the finish on an old tray is quite rough, sand the rough places smooth with coarse sandpaper before applying Japanese tea paper or newspaper to finish. Use methods described in two preceding projects. (See figure 39.)

## GOLD-LEAF NUT OR BONBON BOWL

Such a pretty little dish to fill with sweets or nuts, and rich-looking enough to set before a king! But actually this little treasure was made from the most common dish you have in your cupboard.

MATERIALS

Hard plastic, wooden or ceramic cereal bowl about six or seven inches across
Clean newspaper, white glue
One package of gold leaf (hobby or art supply stores)

Gold leaf adhering liquid, 2-inch special gold-leafing brush
Acrylic paints: black, Chinese red, white titanium
¼-inch China painting brush, old toothbrush

METHOD

1. Tear newspapers into 1½-inch squares.

2. Glue squares with diluted white glue to inside and outside of bowl, turning the top edge neatly by slashing the square that turns over. Dry on wax paper so bowl will not stick if you wish to do both surfaces in one step.

3. When completely dry, paint entire surface of bowl with white titanium.

4. When dry, paint inside and out with one coat of Chinese red. Dry well.

5. Brush adhering liquid hit-or-miss over outside surface of bowl. Let stand until it is tacky or according to directions on the particular brand you use.

6. Place pieces of the gold leaf over the tacky spots using the 2-inch gold-leafing brush. Let dry overnight.

7. Brush adhering liquid solidly on the inside surface and when it is tacky, lift single sheets of gold leaf and cover the entire surface inside bowl. Rub over entire surface carefully with a piece of cotton to remove the excess gold leaf. Let dry overnight.

8. Place bowl on a large sheet of newspaper and spatter lightly inside and out with black acrylic, using an old toothbrush to dip the paint and scraping it with a pencil or stick to spatter the paint. You may use a thin black wash to antique the bowl instead of the spatter if you wish.

9. When thoroughly dry, apply two coats of acrylic matte varnish, drying well between coats.

10. If bowl is to be used as a candy or nut container, the addition of several coats of a clear varnish, such as Pittsburg's Satin Pale Varnish, will make a more durable finish.

## ORIENTAL FOOTED BOWL

If you are lucky enough to have an old footed brass bowl such as this one (figure 40), it can be refurbished to make an up-to-the-minute accessory. If it does not have the brass feet, cork ones can

*Fig. 40 Oriental footed bowl, and the red apple fruit basket and salad bowl.*

be substituted. This one was quite corroded, but after being cleaned up it was antiqued in green and black. Jeweled flower design is red and gold. Bowl measures 8 by 4¼ inches.

MATERIALS

    Bowl, brass or metal or any hard material
    Fine grain sandpaper, if needed for cleaning
    Newspaper, white glue
    Medium thick pre-shrunk cord, three cork balls for feet, if needed
    Acrylic paints: white titanium, red, lime green, black, acrylic gloss varnish
    Gold jeweler's paste, large green glass jewels, Bond cement

METHOD

1. Clean and sand bowl and feet if corroded or rusted. Surface should be smooth and clean.

2. If bowl has no feet, glue small cork balls in three places on bottom.

3. Tear clean newspaper into 1-inch squares. Cover inside and outside surfaces completely, except feet, using diluted glue. Beginning on inside, start at edge and work down toward the center. Let dry, then turn bowl over and glue squares from the edge up to center of base. Bowl edges do not have to be covered by turning squares over because cord will be glued over the raw edges of the paper.

4. When thoroughly dry, paint with white titanium over all. Let dry.

5. Draw pattern for cord outlines on bowl (see illustration). Three large 4-petalled flowers similar to the wild rose were drawn and connected with a curving length of cord around the bowl.

6. Use full-strength glue to cover outlines with pre-shrunk cord. Also apply cord around edge of bowl. Press cord firmly to surface and allow to dry.

7. Paint outside of bowl with black acrylic paint, including cork feet if you have used them, but not the brass feet.

8. Paint bowl inside with lime green. Let dry. Paint design. Flower petals here are red. Dry before antiquing.

9. Make black antique wash and brush over green inside surface, wiping off with soft cloth to give the antique effect. Brush wash over design on outside.

10. When paint is dry, highlight all cord outlines with gold jeweler's paste, also highlight red petals a tiny bit. Let dry.

11. Apply three layers of acrylic gloss varnish over all, allowing to dry between coats.

12. Using Bond cement, glue green glass jewel in flower centers.

## RED APPLE FRUIT BASKET

A stunning bowl for chips, fruit, or what-have-you, and a beautiful accent on patio table or kitchen shelf; it was made from a broken wicker basket. A matching salad bowl is the next project, creating a doubly attractive companion set. (See figure 40.)

MATERIALS

Wicker basket 14 inches in diameter (or any size desired)
Newspaper squares, white glue
Masking tape, Scotch tape

Cord, gold jeweler's paste
Acrylic paints: chromium oxide green, red, black, white titanium,
acrylic gloss varnish

METHOD

1. If basket is damaged, mend it with Scotch tape and glue or whatever is necessary to make a smooth repair. If it has handles, remove them and place masking tape over any pointed or rough edges of wicker.

2. Cut clean newspaper into 1½-inch squares. Use diluted glue to cover the entire basket inside and out with the squares. If the basket is quite rough, glue more than one layer of squares over the surface until it is smooth. Let inside dry before covering outside. Dry well.

3. Glue pre-shrunk cord (quite thick or heavy) around edges of basket (see illustration), using full-strength glue. Accent places where handles were removed as pictured in order to give interest to the design.

4. When both inside and outside are dry, paint with white titanium and allow to dry.

5. Draw three free-form apples inside basket as illustrated (the third apple is behind the salad bowl). To outline apples, glue cord with full-strength glue. Dry thoroughly.

6. Give a second coat of white titanium, covering cord also. Let dry.

7. When dry, paint entire basket with chromium oxide green (or a very dark green), being sure to cover base of cord so no white spots will show. Dry well.

8. Paint apples bright red, covering base of cord inside design with the red. Dry well.

9. Make a thin wash with black acrylic and antique the entire basket including the apple designs, wiping off with a soft cloth to give the desired effect. Dry.

10. Make a mixture of paint using white titanium and red. Dip into paint with a 1-inch brush, wipe off and highlight one cheek of each apple. (You can see this effect in the salad bowl illustration.)

11. Rub gold jeweler's paste on all cord or paint with gold paint.

12. Finish with several coats of acrylic gloss varnish, drying well between coats.

## RED APPLE SALAD BOWL

A heavy, hard plastic bowl, cracked so that it could not be used, was metamorphosed into the lovely matching accessory in figure 40. A pottery or china bowl, chipped or damaged by cracks, could equally well be returned to active service in this way. As gifts, these two matching table appointments would be unsurpassed.

MATERIALS

> Bowl, approximately 9½ inches in diameter and 4½ inches high
> Clean newspaper, diluted white glue
> Medium-size cord, gold jeweler's paste
> Acrylic paints: lime green, cadmium green, red, acrylic gloss varnish, white titanium

METHOD

1. If the bowl is damaged, fill cracks with full-strength white glue, working it in with your fingers so it will dry smoothly, leaving no lumps or bumps. If chipped, soak newspaper squares in glue, wad them up and fill in the chip, smoothing to match the bowl surface.

2. Tear clean newspaper into irregular shapes, varying in size from 1 to 2 inches. Using diluted glue, begin overlapping squares at the top edge of bowl so that half the square can be turned over from the inside to the outside surface. Slash if necessary for a smooth turn. Continue around the entire rim of bowl, then glue squares in circling rows around the inside of bowl until you reach the bottom. When inside surface of bowl is completely covered, allow to dry. When dry, turn bowl upside down and glue squares on the outside in the same manner as inside, covering bowl in circling rows up to the base which should also be covered. Let dry thoroughly upside down.

3. Paint with white titanium inside and out. Let dry on waxed paper if you have painted the edge of bowl first as it will be fairly dry by the time the remaining surfaces of bowl have been painted. Turn upside down after painting and let dry.

4. Draw the apple design on outside surface of bowl. Five large apples will fit nicely around the outside of bowl of this size.

5. Use full-strength glue to outline apples with pre-shrunk cord. Press down firmly so that cord adheres to bowl surface. Let dry.

6. Paint cord with white titanium. Let dry.

7. Paint inside of bowl and leaves of apples with lime green acrylic.

8. When inside is dry, paint outside of bowl with cadmium green or a dark green, being sure to paint the rim edge of bowl carefully so that it does not run down into the lighter green inside surface. Let dry. All should be covered with color now except the apples.

9. Make a thin wash with the cadmium green. Brush over the inside surface of bowl, wiping off with a soft cloth to give the antique effect. Dry well.

10. Make another thin wash using the lime green. Antique outside surface of bowl with this, with the exception of apples. Let dry.

11. Paint apples with red acrylic. Make a "C"-shaped accent on the apple cheek by wiping the paint off while still wet with your finger. Let dry.

12. Accent cord with gold jeweler's paste rubbed in with your fingers, touching leaf centers and apples, also, with the gold.

13. Apply two coats of acrylic gloss varnish, drying well between coats, covering inside and outside surfaces, including design, cord, and all.

14. *Important.* If you intend using your bowl as a salad bowl, you must make the surface waterproof and vinegar proof. Coat the inside surface and also the outside with three or four layers of a good, clear varnish, such as Pittsburg's Satin Pale Varnish. This will give the bowl a clear satiny moisture-resistant finish. Dry well between coats.

# 9.
## BIRDS AND SIMPLE FIGURES

Birds have always been a favorite subject for artists seeking to enhance a room with attractive accessories. Whether it be a small, whimsical owl or a mood-setting, colorful figurine, one of these projects is sure to be a conversation piece. A gift of one of these easy-to-make projects to a bird- or owl-collecting friend would be treasured, and the figurines are theme setters at Christmas time or any time.

### LITTLE OWL

Anyone would love this nocturnal fellow (see figure 41), but why not make one for the new graduate? It tells him you think he's a wise and wonderful bird too.

#### MATERIALS

Plaster of Paris owl (may be obtained at Art Enterprises by Pharis: see Glossary, Brand Names, in back of book)
Clean newspaper squares or paper towels, white glue
Heavy cord, gold jeweler's paste
Acrylic paints: white titanium, black, acrylic gloss varnish
Gold bronzing powder, liquid medium, or
gold paint, turpentine

METHOD

1. Cut newspaper into squares of ½-inch to 1-inch, or use paper towels if you wish more texture.

2. Glue carefully over owl, using diluted glue. Begin at the base and work up to the eyes, leaving eyes to the last. When the rest of the figure is covered, cut paper into oblong pieces that will fit from the center of pupil to outside edge of eye, overlapping to give a sunburst effect (see illustration).

3. When completely covered, brush with a coat of the diluted glue to make sure the paper is well saturated. Push corners down with fingers as they have a tendency to pop up as the owl dries. Let dry thoroughly.

4. Saturate heavy weight, pre-shrunk cord in full-strength glue and outline both eyes with cord as in illustration, pressing down firmly with fingers. Use two strands of equal length so both eyes will be the same size, following the contour of the figure. Cut a smaller length for the beak and glue it on in the same way.

5. Cut two more pieces of cord in equal lengths to form the wings. Glue at sides of owl. Cut a long piece of cord to form a little spade-shaped tail. (See figure 42 showing backs of owl.) Allow loop of spade to hang over as shown when it is glued on. Allow all cord to dry completely before handling further.

*Fig. 41   White and gold antiqued owl.*

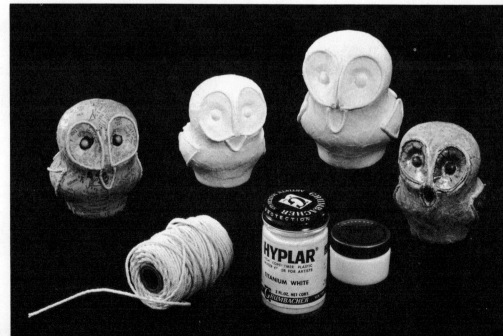

6. Paint with one coat of white titanium, covering paper and cord. Dry.

7. Mix antique wash using gold Venus powder mixed with turpentine. Paint the entire owl including cord with the wash. It will be either a light gold or heavy gold effect depending on how thick you make your wash with the Venus gold, and the turpentine causes the gold to separate into the desired "antique" patterns. Dry well, and handle carefully from now on until the sealer is put on, because the gold will rub off easily.

8. Use ready-mixed gold paint or mix gold Venus powder with liquid bronzing medium to paint cord outlines. Also paint inside cord areas of beak, eyes, tail and wings. Allow to dry.

9. Paint center pupil of eyes with black and add a few small black brush strokes to eyes around pupil.

10. When thoroughly dry, apply two coats of acrylic gloss varnish, drying well between coats.

This method can be used to cover other bird figures such as quail, pheasant, chickens, and so on.

*Fig. 42 The back of little owl showing "spade" tail and wing shapes and a matching paperweight owl and desk tray set.* Created by the author.

## *MATCHING OWL DESK SET

This fun-to-do pair of owls is ideal for a desk paperweight and tray for paper clips, stamps, pencils or what-have-you. The bird is made from a dime store bank and the tray from a china spoon holder. (See figure 42.)

## PAPERWEIGHT OWL

A neat gift for Father's Day or his birthday.

MATERIALS

> Plaster bank from the dime store or Supermarket
> Clean newspaper squares, white glue
> Paint brushes, bowl for glue
> Ordinary string (pre-shrunk)
> Acrylic paint: white titanium
> Gold Venus Bronzing Powder
> Turpentine
> Gold jeweler's paste
> Acrylic matte varnish
> Clear lacquer spray
> Sand

METHOD

1. Cut newspaper squares about ¾ inches square, letting them fall into a small wooden bowl or cardboard box so they won't scatter all over. Read the Basic Formula I at the beginning of the book before you start, so you'll have the steps pretty well in mind and also to get ideas for handling the materials easier.

2. Mix your glue in a small bowl; a small juice can is fine to use for glue and paints because you can throw it away when you are through. Pour or squeeze out glue into your container, then add a small amount of warm water a little at a time to the glue, stirring with the stick until it is about as thin as cream (using about half glue and half water).

3. Take the rubber or plastic stopper out of the bottom of the bank and put it away carefully as you will need it again later when you are ready to put in the sand.

4. Beginning at the bottom edge, leaving the base which has

the hole in it uncovered, glue squares in neat rows around the owl, overlapping the squares in irregular pattern about half way up the owls back and front. If the feet are indented as in the one pictured, care must be taken to put plenty of glue on the square and to press the square onto the foot and into the crevices with your fingers. This is tricky, so watch as the paper dries and push down any that tries to pop up, adding more glue if necessary. At the half-way point, you can give your owl a definitely feathery effect by turning your squares so the corners point downwards, overlapping them as you continue around the owl and up over the head. Leave the eyes for last.

5. When you are ready to do the eyes (owls' eyes are always the most interesting to do because they are so big and round), cut your newspaper squares in half to make triangles or pie-shaped wedges that will reach to the center of the eye, having the wide edges at the rim and the points in the center. Glue these in carefully, overlapping them so that no plaster ever shows through.

6. When the bird is completely covered, stand it on a piece of wax paper and paint it carefully so that no drops run down the figure, with the rest of the diluted glue, pressing down any edges of newspaper that are not tightly adhered to the figure. Allow to dry overnight or as long as it takes to become thoroughly dry.

7. When you are ready to glue on the cord, measure a length around the eye before cutting, and cut it longer than you actually need. Cut another piece the same length for the other eye. Place the cord in your glue dish and pour full strength white glue over it. Lift a piece of the cord up and run your thumb and forefinger down it (holding it over the glue bowl) to squeeze off the excess glue, but leave it well saturated. Place the cord over the outside circle of one eye, cut off excess string and fit the ends together neatly. Press the cord down firmly with your finger so it will not fall off. Repeat with the other eye. Then cut smaller lengths of cord and glue over the inner eye circle in the same way. A short length of cord also should be glued around the beak and around the "ear" feathers above the eyes if your owl has them. The wings of this owl were outlined with the cord from the lower corner of one eye, curving down the side, around the back and up to the lower corner of the other eye. Be sure all cord is firmly glued and that there are no drops of glue running down from it. Allow to dry thoroughly.

8. When the string is completely dry, paint the entire owl including the cord outlines with white titanium. Allow to dry.

9. Mix an antique wash using gold Venus Powder mixed with turpentine, using only a small amount of the gold powder to about ¼ cup of turpentine. Paint the owl with this, including the cord outlines. Dry well. Do not handle much from now on as the gold will rub off until the varnish coat is applied.

10. When well dried, rub gold jeweler's paste over cord outlines with your finger and rub the gold into the small eye circle and the beak. Highlight the owl with the gold paste, touching it up here and there. Let dry.

11. Paint owl with acrylic matte varnish, covering gold cord and solid areas as well as the body. The varnish looks milky when it is wet, but it will dry to a clear finish.

12. When figure is thoroughly dry you can spray it with clear lacquer.

13. Let dry for several days, then turn it upside down and place a small funnel in the hole in the bottom and fill with clean sand. Remove funnel and glue the rubber or plastic stopper in place. Lay owl on its side and place several strips of masking tape over the stopper and the entire base, covering it neatly so that no paper will jut out over the edges. Paint bottom with white titanium, dry and touch it up with the gold paste to match the rest of the owl or leave plain. If you have a piece of green felt, you might cut it to the shape of the bottom and glue it on.

## OWL DESK TRAY

With the owl paperweight (project above) this makes a superb set. The little tray was a ceramic spoon holder found at the dime store. You might find one there or in a hardware store. Or draw an owl figure on an oval dish or tray of similar size. This tray measures 8 by 5¼ inches.

### MATERIALS

Owl-shaped or oval dish or tray
Newspaper, white glue
Pre-shrunk cord or string
White titanium acrylic paint

Gold Venus Bronzing Powder, turpentine
Gold jeweler's paste
Acrylic matte varnish, clear lacquer
Paint brushes, bowl, scissors
Wax paper

METHOD

1. Cut newspaper into 1-inch squares. Turn tray upside down on a clean sheet of wax paper and begin gluing squares, starting at edge overlapping them and working toward center, using diluted glue. When bottom of tray is completely covered, brush with a coat of glue and allow to dry overnight.

2. When it is dry, turn tray over and glue squares to top surface beginning at the edges, turning about ⅛-inch over the edge. Be sure the edges are glued down neatly to the back. Continue gluing squares on the lower half of the owl, leaving the head and eye sections for last.

3. When body section of tray is completely covered, cut wedge-shaped pieces of newspaper to fit eyes around center circle. Fit them very carefully, overlapping a little so that no bare area will show. Glue a round circle of newspaper in the center, covering any uneven points of the wedges, pressing down well. Cover the remaining head, ear and beak area with small squares in hit-or-miss fashion. When front of tray is completely covered with newspaper squares to your satisfaction, paint with one coat of the diluted glue and allow to dry thoroughly on the wax paper.

4. When well dried, saturate cord with full-strength glue and completely outline the outside edges of the tray, pressing the cord down firmly with your fingers. Measure and cut a length to outline the cheek and beak; glue firmly. Also glue cord outlines around the inner eye circle, but not around the outer eye circle or the "feathery" effect of the eyes will be spoiled. Outline a wedge-shaped inner ear area as in the tray illustrated if you wish. For further decoration you might draw a flower in the center of the tray (see illustration) and outline it with cord. Allow to dry completely.

5. When dry, give a coat of white titanium. Dry, turn over and paint the other side. Let dry.

6. Make an antique wash by mixing gold Venus powder with turpentine in a thin mixture. Paint entire tray with this and let dry.

7. Rub gold jeweler's paste on all cord outlines and inside center eye circles. Also inside flower petals if you have made this design. Highlight other parts of owl tray by touching here and there for a rich effect, but leave plenty of the white to show through. It is not necessary to highlight the back of the tray. Let dry thoroughly.

8. Give two coats of acrylic gloss or matte varnish, drying well between coats.

9. Finish with a coat of clear spray lacquer.

## MARGARITA

A charming little figurine, 12½ inches tall, Margarita will add an amusing and colorful accent to any room. Her skirt measures 11 inches across bottom; her hat, 4½ inches wide.

### MATERIALS

Lightweight cardboard (suitbox or shirt board)
Ping-Pong ball, cord, white glue
Thread or yarn cone spool 10 inches high, 3½ inches at base
Gold Gook (see Brand Names)
Japanese tea paper
Acrylic paints: turquoise, white titanium, black, red, blue, flesh
Paper towels
Bowls, brushes, scissors
Masking tape, stapler

### METHOD

1. If you cannot obtain a thread or yarn cone from your yarn shop (knitting yarns come on cones) or dress material shop, make a cone with heavy cardboard, stapling across the overlapped edges.

2. For the skirt: Cut a half-circle with an 8-inch radius from the lighter weight cardboard, by using a compass or a home-made one by tying a string onto a pencil, measuring out 8 inches of the string and holding it at that point, drawing the 8-inch radius with pencil.

3. Fold the lighter weight cardboard circle around the cone from the top, leaving about 1½ inches of the base extending at the bottom. Overlap the circle at the back. Fasten the seam in back with masking tape, securing the skirt to the cone, pressing to round out the sides, giving a flat silhouette. Fasten bottom of skirt front to the cone, also,

with masking tape. In order to retain the flaring curve at the sides of the skirt, place several strips of masking tape across bottom to the outside edges.

4. Cut paper towels into 1-inch squares and glue over lower portion of cone, including masking tape, with diluted (half and half) glue. Also cover entire skirt. Dry.

5. Glue Ping-Pong ball at narrow end for head, using full strength glue. Dry well.

6. Cut the decorative head-piece or "hat" from lightweight cardboard. It should be in a curved boat shape, about 1¼ inches wide at center flaring to 3 inches at the sides.

7. Cover the outside of the hat with paper towel squares, making both edges even. It is not necessary to cover the inside of the hat. Dry.

8. Place headdress on Ping-Pong ball head, gluing with full strength glue.

9. Coat entire figure including the head and hat with diluted glue and let dry.

10. Give one coat of white titanium and allow to dry.

11. Paint dress, hat, and base with turquoise acrylic. Dry.

12. Paint face flesh color. When dry, paint in eyes, mouth, nose, and hair.

13. Decorate skirt with gold lace paper cutouts, gold Gook to outline paper cutouts (as in figure 43), paper cutouts of Japanese tea paper, or use your own imaginative designs. Decorate hat also.

14. Wrap preshrunk cord which has been saturated with full strength glue around the top of neck to cover joining of head and neck, and also an inch lower to create a neckline, looping the bottom strand of cord as shown. Let dry.

15. Paint hands and skirt panels or "sleeves," outlining them with black filling or with flesh color. Or make the hands with gold Gook, bringing them out in relief.

16. Coat entire figure with matte or gloss varnish, depending on whether you wish a glossy or dull finish.

## MADONNA

A decorative treasure to brighten a room or set the mood for Christmas; see figure 43.

MATERIALS

Cardboard suitbox, cardboard tube 1-inch diameter
Newspaper squares, white glue
Heavy cotton or gold decorator rope ⅛- to ⅜-inch thick
Ping-Pong ball, jewels, beads, pearl-headed corsage pins
Gold paper cutouts, masking tape
Paints: acrylic colors
Gold jeweler's paste, Bond cement

METHOD

1. Measure a 12-inch circle on cardboard and cut ¼ of this circle.

2. Form a cone with the quarter circle, fastening the two straight sides together with masking tape.

3. Trace around the large end of the cone by standing it on the cardboard and outlining it with pencil for the base. Cut out the base; attach it to the cone with masking tape.

4. Poke a small hole into the Ping-Pong ball with a sharp pencil or other instrument to fit over small (neck) end of the figure.

5. Glue a 2-inch piece of the cardboard tube to the Ping-Pong ball for a hat, using full-strength glue.

6. With a small paintbrush cover the remaining surface of the ball with full-strength white glue. Let dry.

7. Paint features of face with acrylic paints and allow to dry well.

*Fig. 43  Left and right: two versions of Margarita. Center: Madonna. By Lura Smith.*

8. When features are dry, coat with acrylic gloss varnish. Let dry.

9. Attach the decorator rope with full-strength glue to figure, draping it from the center back down to the base of the front and crossing as in illustration. The second piece of cord outlines the "skirt" and crosses over in back, returning to outline the hem.

10. For the hair which is dressed in two round "puffs" at each side of the head with another at the back, form two 2-inch spirals with the rope, placing full-strength glue on the cord as you work, then glue one "puff" to each side of head and add a twisted knot of rope to the center back to complete the "hair". Dry thoroughly.

11. Paint entire figure and hat, including all cord, with one coat of white titanium. Allow to dry.

12. When well dried, paint hair with black. Dry.

13. Make "crown headdress", cutting it from cardboard. In the illustration you can see the four pieces needed. A high scalloped triangle forms the front piece, held in place by a small curved band. Glue these to the front of the tube with full-strength glue, then

*Fig. 44 Left to right: back view of Margarita, thread cone for base, and back view of Madonna showing arrangement of hair and cord outline. The figure with the wistful expression is Little Boy Angel.*

cutting two narrow, scalloped pieces to be glued in front of the hair puffs. You may have to pin these in place to make them stay. Use common straight pins if this is necessary. Paint with white titanium. Dry.

14. Outline triangle of the face with tiny pearls, using Bond cement.

15. Paint hat, crown pieces and figure and cord with gold Chromotone paint or you can paint all with black acrylic and highlight with gold jeweler's paste when dry.

16. Glue jewels to head dress and front of figure as illustrated in figure 44. A gold or brass chain glued on with Bond cement, with a "diamond sunburst" pin from a piece of old costume jewelry is very effective. Small glass faceted jewels of many colors are used with pearls and odd bits of junk jewelry to make a queenly robe here. Glue small gold paper medallions over rest of skirt, centering them with pearls if you wish.

17. Cut off part of the corsage pins and push them into the back of the hair.

## THE LITTLE BOY ANGEL

This little guy is so cute and easy to make that you can hardly do without him. Did you know that boys could be angels if they tried hard?

MATERIALS

The same as for preceding project except fine cord instead of thick rope, and no jewels

METHOD

1. Cut a quarter circle with a 6½-inch radius out of cardboard (instructions for this are in "Margarita", this chapter).

2. Fasten flat in back with masking tape (see the illustration for shape).

3. Cut a 3½-inch circle from cardboard.

4. Soak cardboard circle in diluted white glue until it is about saturated. Remove and place on wax paper to dry, first crinkling the edges. Watch as it dries, taking it up now and then to crimp the edges again.

5. Form the angel robe by pushing the cone flat, making a flat-

tened oval. Attach masking tape to hold shape. Skirt will extend over base.

6. Cover cone and crimped circle base with 1-inch squares of newspaper, using diluted white glue. Dry thoroughly.

7. Draw wings on cardboard, making them 7½ inches wide at the bottom, tapering to 4¾ inches at top. (See figure 44.)

8. Cut out and glue newspaper squares on wings, front and back. Bend small portions and tips of wings to curve back and allow to dry.

9. When thoroughly dry, outline wings with fine preshrunk cord on the front side only, using full-strength glue. Dry well.

10. Poke a hole in the Ping-Pong ball with a pencil and glue ball to top of cone for head. Dry.

11. Glue cord on robe, outlining the cape as in illustration, and gluing two or three twists of cord around neck for the collar. Glue cord in a swirling pattern down the front panel and around bottom of skirt front and back. Dry.

12. Paint wings and entire figure with white titanium. Dry.

13. Paint head with flesh-color acrylic paint. When dry paint on features and hair. Dry.

14. Paint both sides of wings with gold Chromotone paint. Dry.

15. Paint cape with cadmium green. Paint skirt, front panel and base with rust.

16. Make a thin wash with burnt umber, and when figure is dry antique skirt and cape with the burnt umber wash. Dry well.

17. Highlight all of cording with gold jeweler's paste.

18. Glue wings to back of figure with full-strength glue, with cord to the front.

19. Coat wings and entire figure, including head and base with two coats of gloss varnish, drying well between coats.

## ANTIQUING PLASTER FIGURES

If you like figurines, but abhor the gaudy colors of the inexpensive plaster ones, this method will give you the muted tones and antique look to satisfy the most artistic taste. See figure 45.

MATERIALS

Plaster figures, glue with Bond cement if broken
Newspapers, white glue, cord

Gold braid, small paper or cloth medallions
Paper doilies, gold paint, jeweler's paste
Acrylic paints: gloss varnish, matte varnish

METHOD

1. Paint face and hands with acrylic paint, flesh tone or other, depending on the figure. Since these are Oriental an olive tone was used.

2. Cover the clothing with ½-inch newspaper squares using diluted white glue. When covered completely with the newspapers, brush a coating of the glue over them. Allow to dry.

3. Paint with one coat of white titanium acrylic. Let dry.

4. Paint clothing with desired color. The ones illustrated were painted a grey-green. The base which has not been covered with the newspaper squares was painted the same shade as the clothes.

5. When dry, glue paper lace cutout medallions and decorative braid for the garment outlines and borders with full-strength white glue. Dry.

6. Paint cord, braid, and paper medallions with gold paint. Dry. If cord is to be all painted a color or gold, it may be easier to paint before gluing on to figure.

7. Saturate pre-shrunk cord in full-strength white glue and arrange "wig" or hair on female figure. Press firmly to head and when it is arranged to your satisfaction, allow to dry thoroughly.

8. Decorate pails (as in figure 45) or any accessory with cord using full-strength glue.

9. When dry, paint pails with same color as used for clothing, covering cord also. (These last two steps may be made at the same time as step 4.)

10. Paint thoroughly dried hair with black. Dry.

11. Highlight hair with gold jeweler's paste.

12. Using gold jeweler's paste, antique the entire figure by rubbing on with finger, highlighting complete figure including base and accessories. Or you may wish to use a black or grey wash to antique and tone down the colors to muted tones. If you use the wash, put a little on the face and hands also.

13. When dry, give face and hands a coat of gloss varnish.

14. Coat the rest of the figure and accessories with matte varnish. Dry.

15. Glue felt circles to the bottom of the base.

*Fig. 45  Two antiqued plaster figures.* By Lura Smith.

# 10.

## CHRISTMAS ORNAMENTS AND DECORATIONS

Tired of the same old things at Christmas time? Here are some brand new original ideas for easy papier-mache making, and what is more, they will last for years.

### CRESCENT HOLLY SWAG

For door or mantel, this swag illustrated in color plate is unique, extremely easy and inexpensive.

MATERIALS

Instant Papier-mache mix or Formula II, wax paper
Heavy cardboard, wire for hanging
Several plastic holly leaves for mold forms, about 1¾ inches wide by 3 inches long
Acrylic paints: green, red, white titanium, chromium oxide (dark green)
Gold spray paint
Red satin for bows

METHOD

1. Mix Instant PM Mix according to directions on the package, do not use too much water, about a medium-thick mixture.

128

2. Pat a small amount on the *back* of the plastic holly leaf mold, about ⅛-inch thickness is about right. Have the mixture thinner at the edges and point of leaf. Make about forty leaves, drying well before taking from the plastic leaf mold. Since it is all right if they curl, you can place these in the sun for faster drying.

3. Make about 20, more or less, tiny balls for the berries, about ½ inch in diameter. Let dry.

4. When leaves are well dried, they will pop off the plastic leaves. Paint both sides with diluted white glue and lay on wax paper to dry. Paint berries with glue also.

5. When dry, paint both sides of leaves with dark green acrylic (chromium oxide). Paint berries bright red.

6. Cut crescent shape for the base of the swag from heavy cardboard, masonite or plywood. The dimensions are 17 inches long and 5 inches wide. It is slightly curved at both ends. Paint the base with the same green used for leaves.

7. You will need two holes in the base for hanging. Their placement will depend on how you intend hanging the swag. Insert wire from the back, twisting the cut ends together on the front (they will be covered later by the leaves, and only the smooth loop for hanging will show on the back). Fasten twisted ends to base tightly with masking tape.

*Fig. 46 The leaves of the crescent holly swag are made with Instant PM mix on backs of a plastic leaf mold.*

8. Begin gluing holly leaves onto base front, using full-strength glue. Extend the leaves over the edges so the base doesn't show. When leaves are all glued on, add the red holly berries in clusters of three or more. See illustration.

9. When glue is dry, give leaves and berries two coats of acrylic gloss varnish, drying well between coats.

10. Attach red satin loop-bows to each side of swag.

11. Take out of doors and, with can of gold spray paint, give entire swag one light whiff of gold to highlight entire piece. Don't use too much.

This swag could also be used flat on a table with tall red candles and no bows. Two of them curving down the center of a long Christmas table would be attractive. You may wish to decorate the swag with an attractive red bird with ten long gold tails available in gift and hobby shops.

## NUT TOPIARY TREE

Topiaries are delightful accessories any time of year, but this nut tree (figure 47) is particularly appropriate for the Thanksgiving and Christmas holiday season. With its papier-mache base, it will last for years. The tree stands 18 inches high; it is made on a 16-inch styrofoam cone.

MATERIALS FOR BASE

Instant Papier-mache mix or Formula II
Old lamp base or stand, or use saucer and custard cup
Two tubes Epoxy glue
Acrylic paints: white titanium, Hooker's green

METHOD

1. Combine about a 1-inch mixture from each of the two tubes of Epoxy according to directions on the package.

2. Glue the saucer onto the bottom of the custard cup, centering it carefully. Allow 24 hours to dry before taking next steps.

3. Mix papier-mache. Working on wax paper, pat mixture over all surfaces of the cup and saucer base or the metal lamp base or stand you will use. Make mixture as even on surface as possible. Do not get it bulky or too thick. You can texture or smooth it as

you prefer. Let stand on wax paper to dry.

4. When well dried, give one coat of white titanium acrylic paint. Dry.

5. Paint with Hooker green, or if you wish, give a green antique wash. Make wash by thinning green acrylic paint with water, leaving it fairly thick. This will dry in a mottled effect over the rough texture of the papier-mache surface. Paint the edges and inside the base also.

6. When dry, give one coat of acrylic matte varnish.

MATERIALS FOR TOPIARY

    Styrofoam cone, any height
    Toothpicks, white glue
    Special styrofoam spray paint: green or gold
    Assorted nuts, buckeyes, acorns, miniature pine cones, etc.
    Small artificial fruits, plastic pine sprigs
    Aluminum foil
    Cookie sheet

*Fig. 47   The nut topiary tree and the crescent holly swag (page 128) used as table decorations.*

METHOD FOR TOPIARY

1. Spray the styrofoam cone with special styrofoam spray paint (see Brand Names) as other spray paints will melt the styrofoam material. Let dry.

2. While cone is drying, assemble nuts, cones and all live material you will be using (not plastic fruits, sprays, etc.) on a cookie sheet. Split all English walnuts you will be using and remove the nutmeats. Place cookie sheet with nuts and miniature pine cones in a 250° oven for 3 hours. This must be done to kill any living organisms in the nuts and cones, otherwise the tree will not last any length of time.

3. Stand styrofoam cone on a sheet of aluminum foil and glue nuts with full-strength glue around bottom of cone. Fold the aluminum foil up against the row of nuts to hold them firmly against the cone while drying.

4. When first row of nuts have dried firmly, prop the styrofoam cone on its side with a cup or box holding the tip so that the top is level with the bottom. Using full-strength glue, attach a row of nuts single file from the bottom of the cone to the tip, varying the size and shape of nuts to give interest.

5. Along one side of this row, push toothpicks into the styrofoam beside each nut to hold in place, using two toothpicks for larger nuts.

6. Turn the cone slightly toward the toothpick row, carefully so nuts will not slip, and add a second row of nuts beside the first, varying sizes, shapes and position to add interest. Nestle them as close as possible to the first row, placing toothpicks to hold as before. Let dry for 15 to 20 minutes, then turn cone again and add one or more rows of nuts, using supporting toothpicks as needed. Continue in this manner until the entire cone is covered. Let dry.

7. When topiary tree is completely dry, pull out toothpicks. Where gaps appear between the nuts, glue the tiny artificial fruit in the largest spots, and plastic pine sprays in smaller places (see next step for this).

8. Pull the plastic pine sprays apart and cut each circle of needles in half. Glue these small sprays into all remaining holes, pulling the topiary tree into an artistic whole effect.

9. Set topiary tree on the papier-mache base. It is not necessary to glue it.

10. To clean dust after several years of use and storage, spray with clear plastic acrylic spray.

## CHRISTMAS TREE ORNAMENTS

What could be more fun than making Christmas ornaments with cookie cutters? Young people love helping with these! (See figure 48.)

### MATERIALS

Instant Papier-Mache Mix or homemade mixture (Formula II)
Assorted cookie cutters: Santa Claus, bird, bell, snowman, gingerbread boy, dog, cat, etc.
Acrylic paints: all colors
24-gauge florist's wire, plastic bag, aluminum foil

### METHOD

1. Make your papier-mache mixture according to directions on the bag of Instant Mix or make Formula II in chapter 1.

2. A special "non-messy" method of handling small amounts of mixture is to mix it in a plastic bag and roll it out flat with a rolling pin or pat with your hands to about ¼-inch thickness. Do not make it thinner than this as it will be too hard to handle, but it can be thicker. However, the thicker the figures are, the longer the drying time.

*Fig. 48   Christmas tree ornaments from cookie cutters.*

3. Take rolled out papier-mache from plastic bag, lay on foil and cut shapes with cookie cutters. Use an old silver knife to pull away the excess papier-mache. Smooth the edges with your fingers or the knife edge. Allow to dry completely, checking as they dry as these will have a tendency to curl or warp. Keep turning and flattening the figures to straighten them. Don't rush drying as drying too fast will crack them. Drying time should take two or three days or longer, depending on humidity and weather. If they should crack, however, they can be mended with more papier-mache mixture.

4. When dry, twist wire into a single strand loop and attach to the back of each figure for hanging with full-strength glue. This can be added without glue when the papier-mache is wet by inserting wire into the back, but be sure to bend the ends of the wire to make them hold well.

5. Paint figure front and back with one coat of white titanium acrylic. Dry on a clean sheet of foil.

6. When dry, paint in the desired colors—Christmas Tree, green; snowman, white with black hat, etc. Paint both sides of ornament. Hang on straight wire placed across a cup or glass to dry.

7. Paint entire figure with one coat of gloss or matte varnish.

8. When paint is dry, decorate by gluing on jewels, pearls, sequins, gold and silver braid, beads, etc. if you wish. Or paint on decorations.

## DECORATOR COMPOTE

Another fun-to-make item and, with a little assistance, even a child can make one to use for flower arrangements and fruit during the holiday season.

MATERIALS

Tall, cone-shaped goblet, wax paper
Shallow soup or cereal bowl
Instant Papier Mache Mix or Formula II
Pre-shrunk cord, white glue
Acrylic paint: white titanium
Gold jeweler's paste
Epoxy glue, Hydrastone, container, spoon

METHOD

1. Turn goblet upside down and glue goblet foot to the bowl with Epoxy, following the manufacturer's direction for mixing the cement. Be very careful to center the bowl exactly so that it will not be crooked. Let dry for 24 hours with the bowl face down.

2. Place on wax paper with the bowl still face down and goblet "stem up." Mix Hydrastone (a plaster-of-Paris-like material) in a separate container about three tablespoons at a time, adding water until it is the consistency of very thick cream. Pour the mixture into the goblet and let it set until hard before mixing the next batch. Continue adding small amounts, and allowing to harden until the glass is full. (Adding all of the Hydrastone mixture at one time may break the glass as it heats up while hardening.)

3. When glass is full and the Hydrastone has hardened, cover the entire outside of the bowl and filled stem with a layer of papier-mache mixture, either the Instant Mix or your own mixture of Formula II. Let the smoothed layer dry thoroughly with the compote upside down. Be sure to get both the top and bottom edges of the bowl very smooth.

4. With your fingers run white full-strength glue down a length of cord and glue to the stem in any design you may wish. (See color plate V.) Let dry.

5. Turn compote upright and glue a border of the cord around the edge of bowl.

6. When dry, paint over papier-mache and cord with two coats of white titanium, drying well between coats. Leave inside surface of bowl clear so that water may be used in it for flower arrangements.

7. When dry, highlight the cord with gold jeweler's paste, rubbing on with fingers.

8. Brush with one coat of matte varnish. Dry.

## LARGE DECORATOR CANDLEHOLDER

Here again (see figure 49) is a project using objects found around the house to create a fascinating and beautiful decorator piece.

MATERIALS

Plywood base, 1-inch thick, round, 6¾ inches in diameter (or size to fit your pot)

Old coffee pot, large saucer, interestingly shaped glass jar (this was
a Wesson oil bottle), round glass honey jar, glass telephone in-
sulator, small demi-tasse saucer
Instant Papier-Mache Mix or Formula II
Large cotton cord, about ⅛ to ¼ inch, pre-shrunk
Epoxy cement, white glue
Acrylic paints: burnt umber, burnt sienna
Gold jeweler's paste

METHOD

1. Glue coffee pot legs or bottom to round plywood base with
Epoxy, following directions on the package. Glue the large saucer
to the top of the pot, the oil jar on top of the saucer and the honey
jar upside down on top of the oil jar. Glue the demi-tasse saucer on
top of the honey jar, then glue the insulator to the top of the small

*Fig. 49   The large decorator candleholder; the insulator top is glued to
the small saucer with Epoxy. By Helen Gustin.*

saucer, round side down, thus leaving the insulator hole for the candle holder at the top.

*Directions for gluing:* Use the Epoxy cement, following the manufacturer's directions carefully, and allow each stage to dry thoroughly before gluing the next. It is best to glue the insulator to the small saucer first before attaching the saucer to the honey jar, as the insulator must be held perfectly straight while being glued and dried. In this way, the insulator can be placed with the round portion up and the saucer can be glued on top of it for easier handling. When dry, the complete top section can then be glued onto the honey jar.

2. Mix Instant Papier-mache mix or Formula II. Place a layer of the mixture on the candlestick, completely covering the entire piece. Fill in under the pot if it has legs, so that base will be solid. Let dry slowly.

*Fig. 50  Two ingenious decorator candleholders made from oddments, bottles.* Designed by Helen Gustin.

3. While the layer of papier-mache is drying, dip the thick cord in burnt umber paint thinned with water, so that the cord is completely colored. Don't have the paint too thick as it will tend to destroy the textured look of the cord. Hang cord up to dry, or lay on wax paper.

4. When cord and papier-mache are completely dry, glue cord onto candleholder in a decorative design (see illustration), using full-strength white glue. Let dry.

5. Mix burnt umber and burnt sienna together to get the desired color tone and paint the entire candlestick. Allow to dry thoroughly.

6. Highlight with gold jeweler's paste.

7. Give two coats of varnish—either gloss or matte.

8. Place large candle in top.

Two other candleholders pictured in figure 50 were made from various odd bottles, jars, and cups.

## *UNIQUE DECORATOR FLOWER OR CANDLEHOLDER

The black and gold treasure in figure 51 was designed to hold water for flowers or a very large candle.

MATERIALS

> Glass ashtray, baby food jar, cranberry juice jar (upside down)
> Cereal bowl for the top
> Epoxy cement, papier-mache mix
> Black acrylic paint, gold jeweler's paste

METHOD

The separate sections are glued together with Epoxy cement in the order given above, using the directions for project above.

You can use your own imagination and cement odds and ends of bottles, dishes and jars together to make an endless assortment of these unique decorator pieces. This is not decorated with cord, instead the black painted surface is highlighted with the gold jeweler's paste.

*Fig. 51 A decorative container for flowers—but it could hold a candle.*

## *DECANTER BOTTLE

Another way to salvage a bottle ordinarily destined for the trash barrel is shown in figure 52. These are presents youngsters can make for Dad to decorate his den or office.

MATERIALS

> Glass bottle with large stopper
> Papier-mache mix, wax paper
> Acrylic paints, cord or jewel decoration

METHOD

1. Mix papier-mache. First, working on a sheet of wax paper, build up stopper into any shape desired. Do this gradually a layer

*Fig. 52 The decanter bottle, with and without the paper surface.*

at a time, letting it dry between additions, as it will sag when drying if built up too fast.

2. Cover the bottle, patting on a smooth layer of equal thickness over the entire bottle, maintaining a decorative shape. You may change the shape by building up portions of the bottle, or adding indented panels, or changing the proportions as you go with the papier-mache. If you want a perfectly smooth surface, dry the first coat of papier-mache thoroughly, then make a very wet mixture and work it into the dried coat, smoothing with your fingers. Let dry.

3. Decorate your decanter by gluing on pre-shrunk cord, painting first with white titanium, then with any color you wish. Add jewels, gold jeweler's paste for antique effect.

## MEXICAN MADONNA PICTURE

A picture (see figure 53) which can set the theme for a South-of-the-Border Christmas party. Following these easy directions, you can design your own papier-mache picture.

MATERIALS

Masonite or plywood for background; natural oak frame
Newspapers
Pre-shrunk medium-size cord, white glue
Acrylic paints: white titanium, green, blue, black, red, yellow, flesh,
    purple
Gold bronzing powder, turpentine
Silver jeweler's paste, 3 large jewels
Acrylic matte varnish

METHOD

1. Using diluted white glue, cover the background board of Masonite or plywood with 2 by 3-inch torn newspaper squares. Dry well.

2. Paint entire surface with white titanium.

3. When dry, trace or draw your Madonna design (see illustration), or use any other design.

4. Glue cord over design outlines with full-strength white glue. Let dry thoroughly.

5. Paint inside the cord outlines. In this picture the dress is dark

*Fig. 53   An easy-to-make Mexican Madonna.*

green, the headdress outer portions are blue, center section deep purple, section next to face is turquoise (made by mixing green and blue.) Hair is black, face is flesh-colored and the features are not outlined with cord. When the flesh color is dry, paint the features: upper eye-line is dark blue, other lines of eyes and brows are black. Keep the red mouth quite small as in illustration.

6. The flower petals are silver: rub silver jeweler's paste inside cord outlines with a dot of yellow for the centers.

7. Antique wash background: mix gold bronzing powder with turpentine in a fairly thin mixture. Cover background only with the wash, not the figure. As you paint on mixture the gold will antique itself—great fun.

8. Highlight all cord with gold jeweler's paste.

9. Cover all with a coat of matte varnish.

10. When well dried, glue three large jewels (the ones illustrated are white) on collar.

11. A natural-color oak frame was used for the picture illustrated, but individual taste and decor can dictate the kind of frame used.

## GOBLET CANDLEHOLDERS

Marvelous, translucent candleholders with poinsettias for Christmas, owls for a club or personal motif (see figures 54, 55). Put oddments of candles in them, and use as table appointments—then listen while guests rave!

### MATERIALS

Brandy snifter or other type glass goblet
Paper napkins with poinsettia, owl or other motif
Glass Lustre beads: White, one jar (see Glossary, if you cannot obtain them from your hobby shop or art supply shop)
White glue, sharp scissors
Shallow lid of large box about three times larger than a shoe box

### METHOD

1. Cut out the design (poinsettia or owl) of the paper napkin very carefully with sharp scissors and lay motif aside.

2. Tear the rest of the napkin into small ½-inch squares, separating them as the napkin is usually double or triple thickness.

*Fig. 54  Goblet candleholders decorated with paper-napkin owls.*

*Fig. 55  Goblet candleholders decorated with poinsettias from paper-napkins.*

3. Dilute white wood glue and paint over a small portion of the goblet.

4. Glue squares (be sure they are only a single thickness) to the portion glued, overlapping them a fraction of an inch. Soak the squares thoroughly as you go painting the glass, then dabbing the square with glue so that they are thoroughly soaked. This is the secret to the lovely translucency of the goblet when the candle flame flickers through it. Cover outside only.

5. When goblet stem and bowl are completely covered, allow to dry thoroughly.

6. Glue design over squares with diluted glue. Dry.

7. When design has thoroughly dried, smear full-strength glue very quickly with your finger over the entire paper-covered goblet, then hold it over the shallow box top (lid catches lustre beads, saving them for reuse) and pour the glass glow-beads over it, turning as you pour, covering all areas. At this point it looks completely messy and horrible, but set the goblet in the box lid to dry and *do not try to even out the layer of beads!* Allow a drying time of 12 hours at least. Do not touch the goblet until it is dry.

8. At the end of the 12 hours when goblet is completely dry, leaving it stand in the box lid, rub over the goblet with both hands rubbing off all excess beads. One thin layer of the beads will remain, giving the lovely, flickering translucent glimmer to the candle flame burning inside.

9. Use candle ends or buy votive candles to set inside goblet.

## ANTIQUE PICTURE FRAME

A discarded frame with a hinged stand, shabby and discolored by years of service, can be salvaged and made into a truly meaningful Christmas present. Figure 56 shows it redone as an "antique" frame holding a small painting.

MATERIALS

   Standing frame, with glass if using a photograph
   Newspaper, cord, white glue
   Gold bronzing powder, turpentine
   Acrylic paint: white titanium, matte varnish

*Fig. 56  An antiqued treasure from an old, hinged stand.*

METHOD

1. Cut clean newspaper into ½ - to 2-inch squares, depending on size of frame.

2. Using diluted glue, overlap the squares in an artistic scale-like pattern completely around the frame. Dry well (see illustration).

3. Outline inside of frame with a single strand of cord, using full-strength glue. Glue a double strand on the outside edge of frame. Dry thoroughly.

4. Paint with white titanium.

5. When dry, make antique wash by mixing gold bronzing powder with turpentine in a medium thick mixture. Brush over entire frame and cord. Let dry. This will give an unusual antique texture.

6. Give two coats of matte varnish, drying well between coats.

## ANGEL WALL TABLEAU

The heavenly scene shown in color plate I appears to have been made from antique bronze. It will decorate home or church equally well. Angels are 15½ inches tall (not including wings).

MATERIALS

Old sheet, 12 paper towels per angel
Three sets plaster-of-Paris heads and feet
Clear resin hands or make them with wire and tape as shown
18-gauge wire, masking tape, white glue

Wheat wallpaper paste, floral tape (if making hands)
Gesso, non-tarnishable gold spray paint
Acrylic paints: black, matte or gloss varnish
Aluminum foil-covered board

If you mold the heads yourself from plaster-of-Paris be sure that
2 wires about 15 inches long extend from the neck center for making
the body. Wires about 4 inches long should extend from hands and
feet for attaching to the body frame.

### METHOD

1. *Armature* (or body frame) is 15½ inches high from the top
of head to toe. Two wires should extend from the head to form body
of figure. Add additional wire from hip to form legs.

*Feet* - Attach wires extending from feet to armature wires; wrap
firmly at joints with masking tape. Measure to be sure the body frame
is 15½ inches.

*Arms* - Use two 11-inch lengths of 18-gauge wire. Tape together

Fig. 57   *Patterns for the angel wall tableau; gluing cloth wings to wires also shown.*

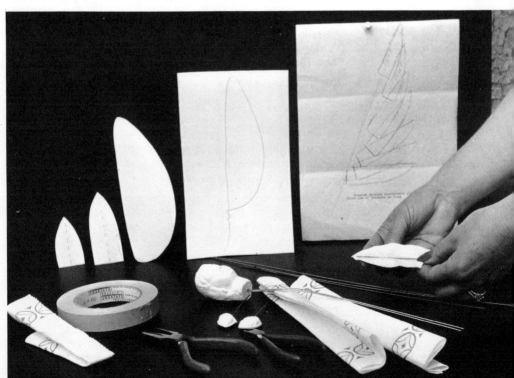

with masking tape at center. Attach to body wires at base of head with masking tape at center, making each arm 6 inches long.

*Shoulders* - To mark shoulders, bend arm wires 1 inch each side of center body making a slight downward bend. This makes the arms about five inches long without hands.

*Hands* - If you use molded hands, fasten to end of arm wires with masking tape and glue. Hand should measure 1¼ inches from wrist to tip of middle finger. If you mold your own hands of resin, drill two holes into wrist end and glue to arm wires.

If you wish to make hands, use wire and floral tape as follows: Form a small pad of floral tape for palm of hand. Cut cord for fingers, glue to palm with full-strength glue. (Let dry on wax paper or foil-covered board.) Wrap floral tape around palm and over base of fingers to make hand. It should measure 1¼ inches from wrist to tip of middle finger. Attach hand to ends of the arm wires.

*Waist* - Mark body wires 2½ inches from neck with masking tape to identify waistline for padding.

*Leg Separation* - Measure 2¾ inches from marked waistline and tape the two body wires together at that point (hip joint). Separate the body wires below the tape to delineate legs. Legs should measure 7¾ inches from leg separation to toe, allowing for a rather long-legged look.

*Knee bend* - 3 inches from the leg separation make a slight bend for the knee. When padding is completed, knees may be raised more when positioning is done.

Armatures for center and side angels are made identically and positioned again after padding and before draping. You cannot re-adjust figures after draping has dried.

2. *Positioning* - should be done now since the wires are the body "bones," then figure is readjusted after padding is completed.

*Center Angel* - One knee is raised about 2½ inches, which will pull up the foot. Keep foot flat against surface so only the knee is extended. (See color illustration to help in positioning.) Arms are extended forward and down slightly.

*Right Angel* - (To the right of center angel in color illustration.) Head should be turned to the left. Right shoulder and right hip are pulled up and turned toward the left, so angel is resting on left hip. Left knee is pulled up 2 to 2½ inches and turned to the left. Right knee is very slightly bent and turned to the left. Arms are extended up and to the left.

*Left Angel* - (To the left of center angel in illustration.) Head should be turned slightly to the right. Left shoulder and left hip are pulled up and turned to the right so angel rests on the right hip. The right knee is pulled up 2 to 2½ inches and turned to the right. The left knee is slightly bent and turned to the right. The arms are extended up and to the right.

Be sure while positioning the armature to keep the thigh and shin parts of the leg wires straight as they are in the bones of the human body. This helps give a graceful pose to the figure.

3. *Padding The Armature* - Cover a heavy sheet of cardboard or a wooden breadboard with wax paper or aluminum foil to give a good surface for working on the figures.

Fold paper towels, either one or two depending on what part of the figure is being padded, into strips ¾ inch wide, folding the long way of towel. You will need at least 12 paper towels per figure, so use a large roll and expect to use most of it for the three angels.

a. Begin at neck. Fold one towel into a strip ¾ inch wide. Wind around neck, centering the strip on the body wire at the base of head. Bring ends of strip forward after winding around neck, and bring end out on each shoulder, securing with masking tape.

b. For the body, use two unseparated towels folded in one long strip. Tape center of towel strip to neck padding at back of head, bring over one shoulder and across to the opposite side. Wrap around body wires to waistline, then back up to neck and over the other shoulder, then back to waistline. Tape padding in very securely at waistline, with masking tape. Repeat with the other end of towel on opposite side.

c. Use one towel for each arm, wrapping from shoulder to wrist. Tape securely at wrist.

d. Use two towels folded into one long strip for hip and thigh area. Attach below waist, wrapping from below waist down to leg separation and back to waist, then back again to leg separation. Bring end down on one leg and tape securely. This will wrap down about 1 inch on leg. Fold two more towels in the same manner and wrap over the previous padding from waist to opposite leg separation and back to waist. You may finish at the waistline or below waistline, depending on how tightly you wrap.

e. Use one folded towel or more on each leg to finish padding to the ankles.

f. Fold one towel into a strip ⅛-inch wide to wrap around the base of hips to smooth and widen them. *Note:* On the side angels, still another towel may be added in this manner to extend the hips.

g. Padded armature should now be completely covered with masking tape. This will prevent the paper toweling from absorbing too much moisture when you are draping the figures.

4. *Draping*

a. Prepare wheat wallpaper paste or liquid starch for your dipping solution. About 6 or 8 cups will be needed for draping the three figures.

b. Lay angel on work board measuring about 20 inches by 15 inches, covered with heavy foil. Carefully position figures again, checking with Step 2.

c. Sleeve - Tear or cut a strip of sheeting 3 inches by 20 inches long. Dip into solution to saturate cloth. Lift out, smoothing off excess liquid, and fold the piece in half the long way to measure 1½ by 20 inches. Start at wrist and wrap strip around arm to arm-pit, allowing folded edge to overlap the raw edge as you go.

d. Robe - Sheeting 18 inches wide by 30 inches long. Measure 4½ inches from each side and make a slash about 5 inches long from the top for armholes. Dip robe in paste and form a 1½-inch hem at the lower edge of skirt by pressing between fingers. Place each side to slash under shoulder back of angel. The center piece

*Fig. 58   Angel wall tableau—wrapping the wire figures of angels.* By Irene Immerick.

is the blouse; gather this at the neckline and squeeze in at waistline. Drape remaining skirt in a graceful manner allowing feet to show. Back of skirt is folded under the body and legs with feet showing just below front hemline. Dip a length of pre-shrunk cord in the paste and place around waistline for belt, tucking ends under body.

e. Oversleeve - Sheeting 14 inches wide and 8 inches long. Dip into paste and turn one edge of the long side making 1½-inch hem. Lay raw edge toward body under one shoulder, bring sleeve down on the board and up over the arm to back of shoulder, concealing all raw edges. Arrange lower end of oversleeve in graceful folds. Repeat for other oversleeve.

f. Collar - Sheeting 8 inches wide and 5 inches long cut on the *bias* of the material. Dip and make a ½-inch hem on the long edge of collar. Carefully lift one shoulder of angel from board and place one end of collar underneath. Pull gently around the front to the other shoulder and secure end underneath. The collar should have soft folds as in illustration.

g. Drying - leave angel *absolutely flat* on the foil-covered board and do not move it until it is dry.

5. *Wings* - Make two for each angel. For one wing: Bend an 18-inch piece of 18-gauge wire into an elongated oval. The straight side (see illustration, pattern 4) will be 9 inches long, the curved side 8 inches with the remaining inch twisted around the base or "stem" of the wing. Cut two pieces of sheeting same pattern as the wire oval but about ½-inch larger over all. Dip these into the paste and place one on each side of the wire, letting them extend ½-inch. Press down firmly. Allow to dry flat on the work board. When dry, trim material to about ⅛ inch from wire edge. (Large pattern #3.)

Wing feathers - For one wing: You will need eleven long feathers (pattern #2) and seven short feathers (pattern #1). More may be used if necessary. Cut patterns from cardboard (pattern #1). These are the short feathers and are 1½ inches wide at the base and 2¾ inches long, tapering to a point. The large feather pattern (#2) should be cut 1¾ inches at the base and 3¾ inches long, tapering to a point. Cut seven short feathers and eleven long ones from sheeting with the cardboard pattern. Dip feather material in paste and place 18-gauge wire the same length as feather down the center, folding cloth over until the edges meet. Press firmly and allow to dry on the foil.

Assembling wing: - When feathers and wing base are dry, lay small feathers on the tip of wing allowing the first one to extend half its length above the tip. Glue with full-strength white glue. Continue gluing feathers on wing, overlapping them as you come down the wing. Make three overlapping rows with smaller feathers at the tip. Finish by gluing one long feather straight up the wing to cover bases of preceding rows. Make the wings in pairs, one left and one right. Allow to dry on foil-covered board.

Attaching to angels: - When thoroughly dry, attach wings by pushing end wires of wings through waist padding, securing firmly with glue and covering with masking tape. The wings may be shaped into a gentle curve and positioned at this time. The center angel uses a left and right wing, the right angel has two right wings, the left angel two left wings (see illustration).

6. *Halos* - if desired. Wrap a 12-inch length of 18-gauge wire around a glass tumbler about 2½ inches in diameter leaving a 3-inch stem (approximately). Glue stem with white glue into wing behind angel's head.

7. *Backing and Hanging Ring* - Cut lightweight cardboard into a shape matching the general shape of the angel body (not wings or head). This is not meant to show so it should be an inch or more smaller than the robe of the figure. It will be attached to the back of robe, body and bottom of wings. Make two holes at the top of backing which will be under the wings, and push wire through holes with raw ends toward angel body. Twist ends together, leaving a loop of wire for hanging on outside. Glue entire cardboard base to the back of angel. Let dry.

8. *Finishing* - When all is dry, coat the entire figure front and back with one coat of gesso. (You may use white glue instead, diluted in the ratio of 3 parts glue to 1 part water. Use three coats of the glue instead of one coat of gesso, drying well between coats.) When dry, spray front of angel with at least two coats of gold non-tarnishable spray paint, drying well between coats. Spray the back of angel at least once. Antique with a wash made with black acrylic paint if you wish. This gives depth and a rich bronze metal look. Finish with one coat of acrylic gloss or matte varnish.

# Glossary of Terms, Materials
# and Brand Names

*Acrylic paints and varnishes*. Water soluble, odorless, quick-drying paints used in papier-mache work and other art work. Best known and used almost exclusively here are Grumbacher *Hyplar* High Copolymer Plastic Water Colors for artists, made by Grumbacher, New York, N.Y. 10001. Also used is Liquitex Acrylic Polymer Emulsion, made by Permanent Pigments, Inc., Cincinnati, Ohio 45212

*Antique wash*. A thin mixture of acrylic paint and water, or metallic paint and turpentine

*Art Enterprizes by Pharis,* 1578 West Lewis, San Diego, California 92100. Manufacturer and distributor of art supplies.

*Bond Cement*. Bond All-Purpose Cement #527. Dries clear. Made by Bond, Jersey City, New Jersey 07300.

*Cabochons*. Unfaceted plastic or glass jewels. (See Jewels.)

*Celluclay*. Ready-mixed dry papier-mache. Water is added for instant papier-mache. Made by the Celluclay Company, Inc., Marshall, Texas 75670.

*Chromotone Gold Paint*. Liquid gold paint made by Sheffield Bros. Paint Co., Cleveland, Ohio 44100.

*Cord or twine*. Hard-twist plumber's chalk line is best. Should be pre-shrunk before using.

*Diluted glue*. Use a well-mixed, creamy solution of one-half water and one-half white glue.

*Elmer's Glue-All.* White all-purpose glue which dries clear. Manufactured by Borden Inc., Dept. CP, New York, N.Y. 10017.

*Epoxy glue.* For extra-strength gluing. Comes in two tubes, one a resin and one a hardener. Manufacturer's directions should be followed. Klenk's Epoxy Glue, made by Zynolyte Products Co., Compton, California 90220.

*Florist's wire.* Very fine wire sold by hobby and variety stores.

*Flower stamens.* Artificial flower stamens sold by hobby and variety stores.

*Gesso.* A liquid giving a hard, china-like surface to objects when painted on and dried. (Hyplar Gesso, Acrylic Polymer Latex Emulsion made by Grumbacher.)

*Gook, the Fantastic Plastic.* Tube of paste-like material which hardens to a plaster-like solid. Used for building up surfaces and making designs. Stock #G5, manufactured by Woodhill Chemical Corp., Cleveland, Ohio 44100.

*Grumbacher.* Manufactures Hyplar acrylic paints, gloss and matte mediums and varnishes used in papier-mache and other craft work. Also makes Gesso, Modelling Paste and Extender, Gel and many other artist's supplies. M. Grumbacher, Inc., 460 West 34 St., New York, N.Y. 10001.

*Hydrastone.* A white powder which when mixed with water and poured into a mold makes a plaster-of-Paris-like figure. Made by Art Enterprizes (see above).

*Jeweler's metallic paste or wax.* A product such as Treasure Jewels Paste or Rub n' Buff.

*Jewels.* Glass or plastic jewels, faceted or unfaceted, obtained in hobby shops or variety stores. Also from Glass jewels, Fitzgerald Enterprizes, Inc., Oakland, California 94600.

*Treasure Jewels Paste,* a metallic wax finish made by Connoisseur Studio, Inc., Louisville, Kentucky 40200. Gold, silver and metallic colors for highlighting. Also see Rub 'n Buff.

*Joli Glaze.* A resin glaze used for papier-mache. Gives a very hard shiny finish seal. Made by Joli, Box 3006, Torrance, California 90500.

*Lacquer.* Any clear lacquer or lacquer spray for sealing.

*Liquitex.* Acrylic Polymer Emulsion, gloss or matte varnishes and paints. Manufactured by Permanent Pigments, Inc., Cincinnati, Ohio 45212.

*Lustre beads.* Tiny transparent beads (sometimes called Glo-beads) stocked in hobby and variety stores. Manufactured by Art Enterprizes (see above).

*Magic Steel.* Similar to Gook, a paste-like material which hardens to a metal-like solid. Manufactured by Magicraft, Magic American Chemical Corp., Cleveland, Ohio 44128.

*Masonite.* A wood-fiber material, pressed in sheets. Used for art work, partitions, insulation, etc. Used in papier-mache craft for plaque backing. Obtain in art stores.

*Modeling Paste.* A smooth, chalky liquid having the property when painted over a surface of drying to a very smooth china-like base which will "build up" with repeated applications. Water soluble. Grumbacher's.

*Papier-mache mix.* Use a commercial instant papier-mache mix or the homemade pulp as in Basic Formula II, page 16.

*Pearl essence.* A liquid giving a pearl lustre when painted over or added to acrylic paints. Obtainable in art shops.

*Plaster of Paris.* Can be found in paint or hardware stores.

*Rub 'n Buff.* A metallic paste finish in gold, silver and colors. Comes in a tube. Manufactured by American Art Clay, Indianapolis, Indiana 46200.

*Shredimix.* Dry, prepared papier-mache instant mix.

*Swistraw.* A raffia-like material coming in many colors which may be crocheted to make flowers, trim for papier-mache jewelry, etc. Distributors: La Jeune, Inc., 1060 West Evelyn Ave., Sunnyvale, California 94086.

*Styrafoam Spray Paint* by Aleene, Temple City, California 91780.

*Tacky.* White all-purpose glue, dries clear. Manufacturer: Aleene, Temple City, California 91780.

*Varnish.* Hyplar Gloss or Matte, Medium and Varnish are used in papier-mache craft. Made by Grumbacher. Pittsburg's Satin Pale Varnish for special waterproof seal. Obtainable in paint stores.

*Venus Bronzing Powders.* Gold, silver and metallic powders to mix with liquid medium for metallic paint, or with turpentine for antique washes. Made by U.S. Bronze Powders, Inc., Flemington, New Jersey 08822.

*Venus Bronzing Liquid.* For mixing with bronzing powders. Made by U.S. Bronze Powders, Inc. Flemington, New Jersey 08822.

*Wallpaper paste.* Can be obtained in wallpaper and paint stores. Comes in dry powdered form. Mix with water to make a starchy paste. One brand is Sunseal Wheat Paste, manufactured for Patent Cereals Sales Corp., Geneva, New York 14456.

*White glue.* All-purpose glue which dries clear and is water soluble, such as Elmer's, Tacky, or Art Paste (by Art Enterprizes), all listed.

*X-Acto craft tools.* Made especially for hobby work by X-Acto Corp.

*Note:* Consult your local hobby or art supply dealer for the products named; if he doesn't stock them, he can order for you or suggest good substitutes.

# Index